▶ Writing Anthropology

Other Palgrave Pivot titles

Robin M. Lauermann: **Constituent Perceptions of Political Representation: How Citizens Evaluate their Representatives**

Erik Eriksen: **The Normativity of the European Union**

Jeffery Burds: **Holocaust in Rovno: A Massacre in Ukraine, November 1941**

Timothy Messer-Kruse: **Tycoons, Scorchers, and Outlaws: The Class War That Shaped American Auto Racing**

Ofelia García and Li Wei: **Translanguaging: Language, Bilingualism and Education**

Øyvind Eggen and Kjell Roland: **Western Aid at a Crossroads: The End of Paternalism**

Roberto Roccu: **The Political Economy of the Egyptian Revolution: Mubarak, Economic Reforms and Failed Hegemony**

Stephanie Stone Horton: **Affective Disorder and the Writing Life: The Melancholic Muse**

Barry Stocker: **Kierkegaard on Politics**

Michael J. Osborne: **Multiple Interest Rate Analysis: Theory and Applications**

Lauri Rapeli: **The Conception of Citizen Knowledge in Democratic Theory**

Michele Acuto and Simon Curtis: **Reassembling International Theory: Assemblage Thinking and International Relations**

Stephan Klingebiel: **Development Cooperation: Challenges of the New Aid Architecture**

Mia Moody-Ramirez and Jannette Dates: **The Obamas and Mass Media: Race, Gender, Religion, and Politics**

Kenneth Weisbrode: **Old Diplomacy Revisited**

Christopher Mitchell: **Decentralization and Party Politics in the Dominican Republic**

Keely Byars-Nichols: **The Black Indian in American Literature**

Vincent P. Barabba: **Business Strategies for a Messy World: Tools for Systemic Problem-Solving**

Cristina Archetti: **Politicians, Personal Image and the Construction of Political Identity: A Comparative Study of the UK and Italy**

Mitchell Congram, Peter Bell and Mark Lauchs: **Policing Transnational Organised Crime and Corruption: Exploring Communication Interception Technology**

János Kelemen: **The Rationalism of Georg Lukács**

Patrick Manning: **Big Data in History**

Susan D. Rose: **Challenging Global Gender Violence: The Global Clothesline Project**

Thomas Janoski: **Dominant Divisions of Labor: Models of Production That Have Transformed the World of Work**

Gray Read: **Modern Architecture in Theater: The Experiments of Art et Action**

Robert Frodeman: **Sustainable Knowledge: A Theory of Interdisciplinarity**

Antonio V. Menéndez Alarcón: **French and US Approaches to Foreign Policy**

Stephen Turner: **American Sociology: From Pre-Disciplinary to Post-Normal**

Ekaterina Dorodnykh: **Stock Market Integration: An International Perspective**

Bill Lucarelli: **Endgame for the Euro: A Critical History**

palgrave▶pivot

Writing Anthropology: A Call for Uninhibited Methods

François Bouchetoux
I-Shou University, Taiwan

WRITING ANTHROPOLOGY
Copyright © François Bouchetoux, 2014.

All rights reserved.

First published in 2014 by
PALGRAVE MACMILLAN®
in the United States—a division of St. Martin's Press LLC,
175 Fifth Avenue, New York, NY 10010.

Where this book is distributed in the UK, Europe and the rest of the world, this is by Palgrave Macmillan, a division of Macmillan Publishers Limited, registered in England, company number 785998, of Houndmills, Basingstoke, Hampshire RG21 6XS.

Palgrave Macmillan is the global academic imprint of the above companies and has companies and representatives throughout the world.

Palgrave® and Macmillan® are registered trademarks in the United States, the United Kingdom, Europe and other countries.

ISBN: 978-1-137-40418-3 EPUB
ISBN: 978-1-137-40417-6 PDF
ISBN: 978-1-137-40416-9 Hardback

Library of Congress Cataloging-in-Publication Data is available from the Library of Congress.

A catalogue record of the book is available from the British Library.

First edition: 2014

www.palgrave.com/pivot

DOI: 10.1057/9781137404176

À Mémé Suzon et en mémoire de Pépé Roger, mythiques fondateurs de notre tribu bellocoise.

Contents

Preface		vii
Acknowledgements		viii
1	Introduction	1
	Taiwan, 2012	4
2	Fire	12
	Western guilt	13
	Structural guilt	15
	No culture	19
	Subjectivity-based guilt	21
	Coping with guilt	25
	No integration: the "lacks"	29
	No integration: the "excesses"	36
	No sincerity	45
	No respect	50
	Idealism	54
3	Water	59
	Ethnogastritis: back to the future	60
	Fieldwork in an advertising agency	65
	Disintegration and miscommunication	70
	Eroticism	76
4	Conclusion	94
	References	101
	Index	121

Preface

Dear anthropologist, student of anthropology, brother, I must warn you before you read further. Some pages in this little book might not be of your liking; perhaps they will even infuriate you, and if they do I would like you to picture my apologising face. Far be it from me to hurt your feelings, or drown you in my stream of consciousness, or worse, put you off anthropology. My more benign intention is to recall some of the challenges inherent in writing cultural anthropology, and to offer a word of caution on the political correctness you are bound to come across in the field. To disturb political correctness, this mundane ingredient of socialisation in no way unique to ethnographic research, is to explore what structures the discipline and therefore respect it. So I request your lenience, dear reader, towards the hesitant narrative that follows. I shall not expect you to embrace my views but to critically evaluate them. Consider what you would accept and reject. I only hope to either shape or confirm your own convictions, whether they converge with, or recede from, mine.

Acknowledgements

I am grateful to my educators and mentors, especially Christiane Goudeaux who taught me French, Michèle Couchouron who taught me Spanish, and Gavin Jack who taught me cultural studies. Lin Tzu-Yen suggested I submit a book proposal. I would also like to thank Robyn Curtis, Erica Buchman and the editorial team; Vidhya Jayaprakash and the production team; and the reviewer for producing an insightful and courteous critique of the manuscript. Let me salute in particular his open-mindedness since despite personal dislikes he consented, against all odds, to the publication of this book. I, and I alone, am guilty for writing it.

1
Introduction

Abstract: *This chapter introduces the book as an essay that calls for uninhibited methods in anthropology. Such methods attempt to turn the inhibitions of Western writers, which originate from the guilt they experience in their relationships with the people they study, into a creative force rather than a burden.*

The first chapter of the book will analyse methodological failures in which issues of reflexivity, reciprocity, sincerity, respect, and integration are at stake. The second chapter will build on this critique through the concept of "ethnogastritis" and outline strategies for integrating and writing the field.

In this introduction, the exoticism of Taiwan hints at the emotional kind of anthropology that the book intends to dwell on, and promote.

Bouchetoux, François. *Writing Anthropology: A Call for Uninhibited Methods.* New York: Palgrave Macmillan, 2014. DOI: 10.1057/9781137404176.0004.

This book is an essay rather than a textbook. Although it deals with methods, it does not offer practical guidance for fieldwork; instead it suggests ways of thinking and writing the field, best read in conjunction with other methodological contributions and of course the monographs you are interested in. Specifically, it calls for uninhibited methods—methods that bypass the inertia of guilt, which in Western culture paralyses so much communication with, and understanding of, people. Brother! Do not be fooled by the peremptory style that permeates some passages. I have crafted them in an attempt to seduce you. As long as they inspire or maintain your idiosyncratic engagement with anthropology, my objective will be fulfilled. Trust me, I have used restraint when expressing my beliefs, without being able to identify what exactly caused such restraint. But it probably has to do with the very pitfalls this book outlines, and at the same time struggles to eschew. My position might appear to you as extreme *in* anthropology, but I suppose it only sketches some of the necessarily extreme positions *of* anthropology, which precisely make it the dynamic and exciting discipline it has always been. Read along, and make up your mind.

The book focuses on *relationships* broadly speaking, on what happens *between* the researchers and the researched. It is divided into two chapters. The first is a critique of anthropology from an existential and phenomenological point of view. It reviews tricky situations where anthropologists for some reason fail to establish satisfying rapport with people, leading them to reconsider what they do, or at least the ways in which they do it. Addressing issues of reflexivity, reciprocity, honesty, and respect, this first chapter suggests that anthropologists set themselves the task of integrating a community of adoption while feeling very guilty about it. Such integration, which they perceive as either deficient or excessive, nevertheless remains idealised in various methodological accounts. The second chapter builds on this critique to envisage strategies for integrating and writing the field. My research in a French advertising agency in 2005 and later experiences in Europe, Africa, and Asia inspired the argument, which harks back to positions explored in the 1980s when interactions between anthropology, literary studies, and philosophy were most intense. I view the boredom and miscommunications of fieldwork, reflected in the awkwardness of confessional writing, as symptoms of a malaise labelled "ethnogastritis." More importantly, the symptoms of ethnogastritis include the seeds of its cure, namely an eroticism of contingency that reveals the prospect of an anthropology relying on emotions, not discourse. I have injected a small dose of ethnogastritis in this second chapter, as a doctor would a vaccine, to rid writing of my own inhibitions and "heal" it. This procedure considers by implication the limits of writing, or what makes writing normal or acceptable. Here in other words, I tend to push writing out of the frame of the readable—extensive descriptions of nausea, in particular, will not go easy on you. They did not go easy on me either, and probably widened the discrepancy between who I am and what I write. Often I cannot recognise myself in what I write. I will probably read this page, later, thinking I have never met its author. I could not claim to plead my own cause, however, without the experimental flavour of this kind of writing. My own practices had to take into account, at the very least, the critique addressed in the first chapter. Further, the manoeuvre is ruthless but essential in that it probes whether everything can be told, and questions the boundaries of intimacy in recounting my actions and desires, and above all that of others.

Dear you, I wish I could see your face and hear your voice. I want to know you, and as you know I am only able to speak first. I already feel guilty about confining you to the role of listener. But I also assume you were prepared to find, when you opened this book, signs of my presence. Besides, this book precisely deals with guilt. So let me tell you a little bit about myself, and tell me, what else can I do? Whether you make something or nothing of what I share with you, you might as well take it and remember that not every gift is from heaven. When I first took an academic position in a British university, a colleague of mine used to tell me about his projects and I would comment on how busy he must be. Then he would often say: "Story of my life!" and I liked this expression, which contained a humoristic detachment from the reality of his life. At the same time, such detachment made me acutely aware of the basic tragedy of human relationships, and therefore of anthropology—I may become "other," but never *the* other. I will never know and feel what my colleague knows and feels. I can only "access" him by means of the stories he is willing to share with me and my imperfect interpretation of his conducts. Furthermore, the story of his life continues but I am no longer there to hear it. I know he is alive, but as his story ended for me, so did our true relationship. I feel guilty of letting this relationship die.

Taiwan, 2012

I write from this beautiful island that has been so aptly called Formosa. A desire for exoticism brought me here, just as it led Victor Segalen to China. It is a land of steep mountains, forests, and dazzling sunshine; of teashops, friendly smiles, sweet aromas, dances, temples, street foods and convenience shops and chopsticks, sweating bodies, songs, rice fields, stray dogs and monkeys and cockroaches, goddesses, lunchboxes, scooters, raging waves, festivals, neon lights, betel nuts, hot springs, karaoke, and colourful fruits and colourful folklore. In this exotic utopia, my Empire of Signs, I have come face to face with myself. And through a dual movement of elevation and elation, I have discovered myself as other *than I am. This movement reworks my memories and rouses bright images of the future. I can look back at the place I come from with the love it deserves; or more exactly perhaps, my imagination becomes this almighty gaze that embraces* from above *the people I cherish, and my old self among them. I am not escaping from the present. I only want to decide it. So it is not nostalgia or homesickness that I feel, but love of home, desire to wrap it with care as a mother would tuck her baby into bed. Nostalgia refers to times past, to an "elsewhen". My mind is rather occupied with an "elsewhere" I know so well and moves on without me right now, perhaps becoming unrecognisable. Such nostalgia of the present, if you like, empowers me. My feeling of being-in-the-world* (Dasein) *eternally returns in different forms depending on my location.*

I came to Taiwan to unburden myself of my certitudes and reinitialise my system, to unlearn and relearn, to doubt again and therefore think again and exist again (dubito, ergo cogito...). *The "postmodern" vogue in the 1980s and 1990s has been very keen on doubt, building on the heritage of Marx, Nietzsche, and Freud—our great "masters of suspicion" in the words of Paul Ricoeur (1969: 149–150). Doubt had pervaded the spirit of Taoism long before them, and I like to persuade myself that the teachings of Chuang Tzu unconsciously shaped my desire to alight here. I am very suspicious of this thing called knowledge, and the* Tao *moves me (emotionally and physically). I have sympathies for concepts of critique and resistance, but also believe they acquire full significance in the context of voyage, on a tantalizingly slow and sometimes painful path to intellectual maturity, across an unknown land full of obstacles. I wander around, spend time with people, with monkeys, perhaps understand some, and misunderstand most. Trampling on my convictions, I strive to unshackle myself from the yoke of my self and think of the people I would need to live for. Erratically, I meditate on the human condition. The*

Human Condition—Hannah Arendt's ambitious project and French title of André Malraux's historical novel that takes places in Shanghai, not far from Kaohsiung where I write these lines, over there, near me, near us. Arthur Rimbaud, Walter Benjamin, and Jack Kerouac among others valued nomadism and flânerie for no other reason than that they enable us to think of what links us to each other. We do not make a trip, the trip makes us.

I have left one life behind and was reborn here in the R.O.C. (Republic of China). My identity was not eroded or rejuvenated—it metamorphosed. The "Alien Resident Card" equipped my new self with the wings of the official, long-term Other, thanks to which I flapped my way out of the chrysalis. The word "alien" is rooted in the Latin terms alior and alius ("other") and its derived forms alienus and alter, which led to "alienated" and "alterity," as well as the French term of ailleurs ("elsewhere") (Michel, 2004: 5–6). Ailleurs is one of my favourite words, not just because it refers to a vague and possibly exotic elsewhere that I can only imagine at this instant, but also because the connecting adverb d'ailleurs does not translate well into English and must be assassinated as frequently as it pops into my mind, thereby making me Other and situating me Elsewhere as I write in English. Satisfying translations of d'ailleurs are difficult to find in Asian languages and even among Romanic idioms, save perhaps Brazilian Portuguese (aliás); an awkward "for that matter" seems to be the best equivalent (Hagège, 2012: 170–171). To travel is to become Other, to get out of oneself, in other words experience the ecstatic (ekstatikos, "unstable," "out of-where I stand") or the "Different" (Divers) with which Segalen (1978: 41, 75, 99) defines exoticism. Exoticism refers to an entrancing feeling of otherness that follows the "Law of essential Bovarysm" through which I, through my very conception of myself, may only conceive of myself as other than I am. And I delight in such otherness, in such alienation of myself.

Travelling creates a spatiotemporal rupture, that of pilgrimage and its sacred rituals and playful celebrations (e.g., Moore, 1980; Graburn, 1983; Urry, 2002; Amirou, 2012). I live a secular existence at home; but as soon as I travel, as soon as I find myself a stranger among strangers, I open a door onto the sacred (van Gennep, 1981: 16). Even at home I can daydream—my most common experiences of space are enchanted. I see the invisible and statically travel. "To practice space," Michel de Certeau (1990: 164) tells us, "is thus to repeat the joyful and silent experience of childhood; it is, in a place, to be other and to move toward the other." Exoticism is this feeling of young children discovering our mysterious world (Segalen, 1978: 63). Older children create "other spaces," real utopias that are absolutely different from their surroundings (huts in the forest, in the bedroom) and best epitomised in the ship (Foucault, 1994a, 2004). You *and I see the world in different shapes and colours, and the imaginative ways in which we do it have captivated literature from German Romanticism to the eccentrics who were classic names of my French education—thus Raymond Queneau writes Zazie's wonder in the underground, or various accounts of the same scene in a bus; Antoine de Saint-Exupéry, Boris Vian, or André Dhôtel bring the imaginary and the wonderful, hidden in reality, into the daylight; and in most of his works Georges Perec thinks of space as a constant reinvention of the everyday. The exotic, Georges Condominas (2006) tells us on the basis of his fieldwork in Vietnam, is "quotidian," everyday practice. We envisage the possible, and anticipate its realisation. We imagine alternative arrangements of places, and plan our behaviour accordingly. Comedians on a stage we contribute to create, we carefully manage our emotions. We design our self-presentation depending on circumstances. Our relations with people are theatrical (c.f. the famous theme of the* theatrum mundi *developed by Goffman (1959) in sociology). This competence we have in skilful acting develops outside theatre in everyday life, in what Honoré de Balzac called* The Human Comedy. *And what best illustrates our practices of self-control than the so-called "poker face"?*

I swapped my unpronounceable names for Lin Fan, because lin (林) *means the forest, as my surname probably used to, and because the easily drawn* fan (帆), *the sail, very roughly sounds like the first syllable of my first name. Besides, the sail connotes the epic travels of explorers. Introducing myself as Lin Fan caused much hilarity in the classroom, where I learnt that Lin Fan was a female Malaysian singer, and only the different writing of her* fan (凡) *cleared me of imposture. I had quite literally become someone else. In a chapter entitled "What's in a Name?," the anthropologist Michael Jackson (2005: 89) has taken an interest in the other Michael Jackson, the King of Pop, not just because of the shared name but "because the role of magic in his life illuminates the role of magic in our own." Lin Fan, the celebrity, need not open my eyes to magical operations in my own life—choosing her name already did the trick. Imagine my luck! I have become a star by serendipity. Why would I complain about my rebirth under a lucky star, under the spotlights? Let it shine on me, I am willing to dance and sweat with mock pride! When I see people dancing outside, in squares and in parks, on campuses and beaches, they fill me with joy. This joy is all the more acute since dancing has more or less disappeared from my own society. I wonder why so many Western societies have relinquished the rituals and sense of community reminding us that life is worth living, and thrown themselves into a whirlpool of sadness. A culture that is no longer able to dance must be terminally ill (Piolat, 2011: 16–20).*

Before I first landed in Taipei, I had read in a tourist guide that Taiwan was "one of the most welcoming countries in the world." The statement put a smile of excitement tinged with scepticism on my face. Then I realised how true it rang. It hits me every day. In the city, in the forest, on the beach, I smell and taste friendliness. I inhale it with the scent of flowers and boiling broths, and suck it with the salt of sea spray against my lips. On a Sunday evening in November, I bump into a couple on a tiny artificial island. It is already dark and I only make out some of their features. They invite me to sit down and we quietly experience the serenity of the lake, hardly disturbed by the buzzes of insects, the croaks of distant frogs, and the laps of ripples against the pillars beneath our feet. Nature cradles us and we almost doze off, drift into dreams. Our three sitting shadows grow fainter as we leave reality. Images blur—I see myself on my father's rowing boat at dusk, absorbed in a soundless euphoria of solitude and communion with the Dordogne River, and imperceptibly drifting on its black waters as if waiting to fade or evaporate into the feathery mist that surrounds me. I look down to the lake that glistens under the moonlight, and feel a velvety touch inside my ear, an unidentifiable whisper between vibration, voice, and music. It must be the wind dropping a classic line of poetry in my schooldays: "O time! suspend your flight" (Lamartine). At last its lyricism makes sense! The man sitting on my right yawns, I feel a cold smoothness on my skin, and I look up at the man, who has just nudged my arm with this citrus fruit called kumquat. We eat the kumquats from a plastic bag. Munching on their sweet sourness in the silence of the night, we gaze into the distance and the breeze makes us squint ever so slightly.

Perhaps I left my own community to fully experience another, which could have been mine, and understand my luck. I needed to empty myself before I could be full again. Throw up my referents and discover new dishes, as well as new ways of savouring them. Every day I must grab knowledge with chopsticks, learn from local life, bond with others. Roger Caillois (1993: 167) says that we seek out fullness and reunion in celebrations. I witness the arrival of Matsu, goddess of the sea, in the vicinity of Taichung. She is the highlight of a colourful parade of gods, ghosts (who can be promoted to gods if they behave, according to the Taoist tradition), and illustrious characters. I get swept away with an elated tumult of whistles, drums, gongs, cymbals, and speakers blasting traditional music, and chants, and sounds of real flutes played live. From time to time, even louder fireworks manage to muffle this cacophony. The smoke spreading from incense sticks and firecrackers obscures my sight. Some pilgrims try to divert Matsu away from her itinerary towards their own temples, grasping and pulling at the arms of her carriers, who wear outsize and flamboyant

DOI: 10.1057/9781137404176.0004

masks that impersonate gods. The procession is extravagantly beautiful in the manner of Kon Satoshi's Paprika whose dreams replicate some of its aspects. Some people have downloaded a "Matsu tracker" on their mobile phones, which indicates her exact location via the GPS. The application is useful since she was four hours behind schedule when I saw her. As the goddess approaches in her portable shrine, the crowd gets more excited, the shouts more deafening. Here and there, trays filled with fruits and sweets—offerings! An endless queue of people has prostrated itself on the ground and I lay somewhere along the queue. We all wait for the shrine to pass over our heads and bless us. Days later Matsu will be back in Dajia, her point of departure. The Matsu festival is a major pilgrimage in our world, and a frantic whirl of pleasure. The following day in a neighbouring town, I come across other rituals linked to other deities. A man in a sacred costume drinks a potion and writhes in trance. Not far, others flog themselves. The closest temple is home to the god of drunkenness who, more than most, knows that in vino veritas, or—in its Chinese equivalent— "after wine blurts truthful speech." I shiver with delight.

On the road to Meinung, at twilight, from an abandoned temple overlooking the Kaoping River, the beauty of the landscape brings tears to my eyes. I cry like the baby discovering the world. I surrender to the aesthetic emotion that these colourful layers awaken in me—the murky grey of the riverbank, the pink clouds, and, rising above them in the Pingtung County, the dark green of floating mountains whose calligraphy of lumps and peaks borders the orange immensity of the sky. Here I decide to worship the sun, and the planet I owe my life to. I take refuge in a pagan prayer, a confused incantation, for I cannot transcribe into words the succession of evanescent reminiscences and dreamlike images that imprint on my mind. The reality I see fuses with my memories and fantasies. I like Murakami Haruki's writing of such experience through parallel worlds, in Hard-Boiled Wonderland, The Wind-Up Bird Chronicle, or 1Q84, for example. And I have pictured the mysterious "Dolphin Hotel" of his Dance Dance Dance as the "Grand Hôtel Moderne" in Saint-Sernin-sur-Rance (France), which for me embodies the same fantastic reality, for I spent many holidays as a child in this disused family hotel where everything belonged to the past, where a magic flavour of time travel permeated every corner of the edifice. I remember the shiny grey stone stairs, the creaking parquet corridors, the ghost floors, the room I shared with my brother, our bedside book (La Main Verte, forever lost), the impossibly old bathtub, and kitchen sink, and damp cellar, and our favourite barroom complete with alcohol counter, branded ashtrays, wooden chairs, and massive mirrors. This area was large enough for my brother, my cousins, and me to cycle in it, and reinvent it as our playground. Marcel Proust paints Combray with the intensity of a trance. What the Search of Lost Time means, for him, is really a search for lost places. Just above me Kuan Yin, the goddess of mercy, flashes a motherly smile at me. "Yes, you remember this happiness," she seems to say. Water streams down the white stone carvings of the slope at Kuan Yin's feet, and two dragons play in it. Dragons, protectors of the essential, please preserve my memories! Glide against me, wind round me, choke me, squeeze me like a kumquat, and my love of the Taiwanese will spray out and penetrate their pores, you know that the same warmth oozes from them. Dragons! The declamations of Céline and Gide and Baudelaire bang and ricochet in my head, Chinese characters die in my mouth, and I blurt out an unintelligible mantra of my desire to know the world. Dragons, can you hear how much I would like to ride you and see the world from above?

A place calls to mind another, and another. After an arduous climb in my most unforgettable dream, I reach an abandoned train station that I know in reality, but now set high up in a mountain and sporting elements of a classic novel for French teenagers (Le Grand Meaulnes). From this vantage point many sites can be seen, side by side—a city, fields, the sea, another chain of mountains. This panoptic fantasy creates a dizzying impression of spatial domination that puts my own relation to these places into question.

Dear anthropologist, my faceless addressee, my kin, why would you want to know all this? And what exactly is "this"? Where are the people? What are their names? Why am I not writing about them? Clearly, you have sensed it, this book will not deliver a report from the field, even though it borrows fragments from it. I have produced a monograph elsewhere, which does grant people the weight they typically have in anthropology. I attempted with this monograph to deliver a thorough description of people and their work in an advertising agency. The more I described however, the guiltier I felt. This was not what they said and did, but what *I* said they said and did. Writing Anthropology dwells, in a way, on this difference and the questions it raises: Why do anthropologists write the way they do? What happens between them and the people they meet? How do they deal with alterity? The motivations underlying this book were epistemological, rather than anthropological strictly speaking. I have chosen to open the discussion just as I will close it, with what links us to others, with what we all share, and yet like dreams only concerns "me," the *individual*. I have chosen to begin with what I cannot express for you, and what you cannot express for me—emotions.

DOI: 10.1057/9781137404176.0004

I have just mentioned some of the spatial impacts that Taiwan has had upon me. If I decide to silence them and "focus" on human communities, how reliable will my account of the "Taiwanese" (whatever that may mean) be? Anthropology is often understood as the study of people, of their practices and systems of meanings. But this study would not be possible without an overarching, deep experience of space. By "deep" I mean that overlapping "perceived" and "lived" spaces (Lefebvre, 2000) shape a sensual experience that alternates between different states of consciousness. Thinking the physical realm (*res extensa*) as separate from the realm of consciousness (*res cogitans*) is in this respect counterproductive, since we come back and forth to places that are neither wholly subjective (we see them and record their characteristics) nor objectively real (we visualise them, read them through the prism of other places dear to us). I have begun with my own impressions of becoming an integral part of the environment, not just to situate the author in terms of sensibilities and beliefs, but to imply that distinctions between humans and non-humans, and between nature and culture, hamper thinking. Actor-Network Theory tells us that history is not limited to people, that it comprises natural things affecting our feelings. Places make us who we are. They seemingly only provide a backdrop for our identities, but in reality produce these identities. They encompass a wealth of information that we connect to our mental images, to past places, utopias, *déjà-vus*, and emotional outbursts that can never be eloquently expressed. This chaotic imagery inside us is stimulated by the outside, by what space hurls at us. We fuse with objects and people; we melt with nature, with architecture, with the décor; we turn into objects while objects come to life. Where I am, I have come to understand, is also who I am. And I have never seen the world as I see it now.

The notion of "science" usually involves a relation to the truth of the external world, and that of "literature" to the truth of our internal world. But if space enables thinking in the way outlined above, the distinction can be misleading. And other disciplinary boundaries according to which history tells when and how, anthropology tells who and how, geography tells where and how, and philosophy asks why, may prevent researchers from seeing the forest for the trees. Because in the end, "everything" is literature-science: the epistemological questions of how we know and write the world are *stylistic*. The tentative suggestion this book makes, then, is for anthropologists to consider in a fever of paradox and creative destruction whether their research is not excessively anthropocentric. With this aim in mind, the "water" chapter brings the emotional character of anthropology into sharp relief. Emotions give birth to the non-language of poetry, for example—with poetry language dies to catch a glimpse of our internal life, of the incommunicable sensations that bewitch us and could explain, we feel, "the world."

2
Fire

▶

Abstract: *This chapter analyses relationships between the researchers and the researched. Guilt affects such relationships in essential, structural ways—postmodern reactions to the excesses of classic anthropology deliver new practices and writing styles, but the discipline still relies on autobiographical techniques that do not free it from guilt.*

Reflexivity is a strategic device through which anthropologists cope with their guilt regarding integration. Integration is both lacking (as reflected in boredom and loneliness in the field, and disappointing descriptions) and intrusive (as reflected in spying and camouflage games in the field, and disappointing reciprocity).

The chapter concludes that relationships cannot be sincere enough and respectful enough to make the idealism of populist ethnography come true.

Bouchetoux, François. *Writing Anthropology: A Call for Uninhibited Methods.* New York: Palgrave Macmillan, 2014. DOI: 10.1057/9781137404176.0005.

Western guilt

I am not the perfect ethnographer; Neither am I the perfect son, teacher, boyfriend, and so on. The guilt of anthropologists is not different from ordinary existential guilt. Unlike other thinkers in the humanities or social sciences however, anthropologists face a particularly salient crisis that results from the historical roots of their discipline (colonisation), and from its methods (a style of knowledge production based on memoirs or journals). So guilt is normal, healthy, and not unique to the field experience; but it also drives anthropologists to muse on their own failures and the limitations of human interactions. Where does guilt come from? Important works in Western literature, from The Book of Job in the *Old Testament* to Kafka's (2000) *Trial*, Dostoevsky's (1992) *Brothers Karamazov*, and the existentialisms of Sartre and Camus, reflect the significance of guilt in the Judeo-Christian tradition. Guilt, it is assumed in more or less pessimistic ways, is simply human and as such inescapable. Whether we cause evil, or due to selfishness fail to thwart it, we can never feel completely free from guilt. "Each of us is guilty in everything before everyone, and I most of all," declares Markel in a much quoted passage (Dostoevsky, 1992: 245). Whatever I do, in other words, I am potentially guilty. Drawing on the works of Emmanuel Levinas, Pihlström (2011: 16, 47, 121) suggests that I tend to treat my fellow beings as mere "means," in Kantian terms, and therefore must ask myself whether my own existence is justified. My being there makes me suspect already. But while I think of meaningful, life-enhancing activities, everywhere people suffer. Through this meaningless sufferance I realise that there really is no meaning in life, and that I am also guilty of this situation since what I am writing will not change it. Whether I denounce or lament the poverty and illness that I am shown, am I not giving in to my own introspections and falling into complacency (Boltanski, 2007: 184)? And what else can I do?

Guilt has not only instituted the Judeo-Christian tradition of the original sin, but also Freudian psychoanalysis. *Totem and Taboo* positions guilt at the root of our psychic development and civilisation (Freud, 1998). In the 1950s, Melanie Klein (1975) attributes the anxiety that the eight-month-old baby feels towards broken objects to guilt about her own aggression against the mother's breast. Infantile guilt can be linked to illusions of threatening a good object, or creating a bad object. Ciccone and Ferrant (2009: 73–74, 97–98) comment that sophisticated forms may develop in adulthood, namely "fantasies of guilt" through which the individual believes she is responsible for her trauma, even though she has by no means caused it. These fantasies aim to mitigate the impact of trauma within an appropriation of the event, whereby the individual reinserts herself as the active agent of what she passively endured. Hence a great deal of medical practices, in their effort to free patients of guilt ("this is not your fault, it was an accident"), paradoxically make it worse as they suppress this possibility of appropriation. To be sure, it is essential to tell the patient she is *not* guilty—but this is not *enough*. She must hear the extent to which she feels guilty. This chapter intends to give a voice, in such therapeutic fashion, to the guilt of anthropologists.

The distinction between guilt and shame is not always analytically sound. Thus Ruth Benedict's (2005) opposition between Japanese shame and Western guilt has been widely criticised. The very words that express these closely related feelings do not have identical resonances across cultures. Ōe Kenzaburō (1981: 104) observes that in French literature for example, humiliation and shame represent "the sharpest moral barbs to pierce the heart of both author and reader," while such concepts never appear with comparable force in Japanese literature. Psychiatry usually associates shame with melancholia, and guilt with depression. Guilt results from the experience of losing or damaging the loved object, whereas shame occurs when one feels lost or damaged because of this object (Ciccone and Ferrant, 2009: 7). Focusing not on individual traumas but on intercultural communication, this chapter will revoke the distinction along the conclusions of Norbert Elias (2000: 442–443), who explains that changing social relations throughout history fashioned embarrassment, guilt, and fears of being overcome by our own affects. In anthropological research, such feelings are induced by others—natives, friends, peers, etc.

In the Taiwanese classroom, Lin Fan feels very guilty. First there is the very bad food for thought that he is expected to teach. For example, much of his Human Resource Management *textbook contains boring commonsense, or worse, reductionist and flawed and ideological discourses on business (e.g., Grey, 2009). Second, there is this strange situation in which the white teacher tells Asian kids that they must learn white culture, while Asian kids are hardly ever keen on telling the teacher what he would love to know about their culture. Instead, they welcome Western knowledge as necessary wisdom and the hegemony of the English language as fatality. No better adjective than "colonial," perhaps, describes such a situation. No wonder Lin Fan feels a bit like*

Tintin in the Congo, *who on p. 36 teaches a small class of pupils—they are as black as the blackboard (Hergé, 1993).*

Structural guilt

Ethnogastritis

I love travelling and hate explorers. When I read their writings, when I learn about their adventures, I either envy them or despise them. No middle ground. I might as well state that I love and hate anthropology, if you will excuse the awkwardness of this formulation that merely intends to evoke the ambivalence of passion. The flames of passion, in Gaston Bachelard's (1973) creative reverie, simultaneously protect and destroy us, purify and consume us. Stirred by the acumens of anthropology I fly too close to the blazing flaws that have plagued the discipline, and get burnt. Fire and fieldwork share the same contradictions. Time and again, warm intentions in the field deteriorated into incendiary destructions. But with sufficient imagination anthropology was able to renounce the certainties of science and rise again from its ashes, phoenix-like, resettling in the imbroglios of politics and the musings of poetry. Before I may comprehend fire, Bachelard tells us, I must dream about it. So let me dream and imagine fieldwork via a parable of guilt I came across in "Nausea 1979," a short story by Murakami Haruki (2006). In it, the person addressing Mr. Murakami vomited every day for forty consecutive days after sleeping with his friends' partners. Painless but undoubtedly anxiogenic, nausea discloses repressed feelings after illegitimate lovemaking:

> So, what you're telling me, Mr Murakami, is that my own guilt feelings—feelings of which I myself was unaware—could have taken on the form of nausea or made me hear things that were not there?

Guilt materialises *ex post facto* in its abject form, as if transgressions had been indigested. Caught in the dilemmas of participant observation, that is a sense of belonging without truly belonging, anthropologists are subject to the same kind of indigestion. I shall label their condition "ethnogastritis" and explore it through the prism of guilt first, and then beyond guilt towards fruitful mechanisms of creative destruction.

Classic anthropology as original sinner

The historical development of anthropology is very much characterised by the repeated failures and dissatisfactions of fieldwork, which forced a few generations of scholars to reinvent themselves. Pervading contemporary writing is the guilt, or shame—to revoke Ruth Benedict's (2005) distinction—rooted in the burdensome heritage of the colonialist venture. Perhaps anthropology's complicity in engineering colonialism has been overstated (MacCannell, 1992: 289). But anthropology did emerge in the 19th century from a posture of "othering" that intensified alterity. People were not seen as subjects or *alter egos*, but as radically different species. Various forms of evolutionism, that is Darwinism (Edward Burnett Tylor, Lewis Henry Morgan, James Frazer, Franz Boas ...) and functionalism (Bronislaw Malinowski, Alfred R. Radcliffe-Brown, Edward E. Evans-Pritchard, Meyer Fortes ...) directly informed and rationalised British imperialism. They promoted, in particular, the idea of a natural and evolutionary time on which all societies were placed—the "civilised" upstream, and the "primitive" downstream. This naturalised-spatialised time gave meaning to the distribution of humanity in space. The faraway savage lived in *another time* (Fabian, 1983: 17–18, 25). French colonies, by contrast, rarely called upon ethnologists as experts (Olivier de Sardan, 2005: 42) and the "structuralist" works by Claude Lévi-Strauss in the 1950s and 1960s had a preference for identifying invariants across cultures. However, Lévi-Strauss (1955: 81) did commit Fabian's temporal error, suggesting for example that lifestyles in the tropics persuade one that "rather than crossing vast spaces (...) one has imperceptibly stepped back in time." Twenty years later Napoleon Chagnon (1974: 197) wrote along the same line that people might become anthropologists when they find it "appealing to speculate about the goodness of fit in another time and another place." To travel is to turn the clock back for Bruckner and Finkielkraut (1979: 75), to "pop up in the 18th century, the feudal age or the dawn of time." Countless other examples could show that this conception has hitherto survived.

Postmodern reactions

In the 1970s postcolonial studies decried anthropology's embedment in several power asymmetries between Western and non-Western worlds (Hymes, 1999; Asad, 1973; Said, 1978), which along with the interpretive and symbolic anthropology of Clifford Geertz, Victor Turner, and

Marshall Sahlins, paved the way for the political awareness (e.g., Spivak, 1988) of a more critical or "postmodern" anthropology in the 1980s (e.g., Rosaldo, 1993). The year 1986 was something of a turning point in the United States, with the publication of three edited volumes that outlined the postmodern critique (Clifford and Marcus, 1986; Marcus and Fischer, 1986; Turner and Bruner, 1986). Anthropology was guilty, in essence, of relying on its own Western supremacy whose *vision* (disregarding other senses) produced colonial perspectives—parochial and pseudo-universal discourses that featured others in timeless, spatially bound and immobile cultures, spoke for them, and silenced them.

Anthropology and geography deplored in comparable terms the consequences of Western "visualism" (Fabian, 1983) or "ocularcentrism" (Ó Tuathail, 1996). Western visual culture, rooted in the invention of the alphabet and philosophy in Ancient Greece (especially in Plato's concept of "idea"), intensified with the revolution of printing technology during the Renaissance. The Renaissance gave rise to the "scopic regime" of "Cartesian perspectivalism" (Jay, 1993), which associates *seeing* with *knowing*. A basic etymological detour reveals at once the linguistic equivalence between Descartes' "I" (*cogito ergo* sum) and the "eye" from which I cogitate and attain knowledge (cogito *ergo sum*). The Greek *idein* (to see), the Greek and Latin *idea* (look of a thing, or archetype), or again the Latin *video* (I see) connect understanding to seeing: "oh, I see" in English, "*ya (lo) veo*" in Spanish, "*je vois*" in French, etc. Or again, as Gregory (1994: 16) recalls, theory is composed of *thea* ("outward appearance") and *horao* ("to look closely"). Such connections lack relevance in Mandarin, Japanese, and I suppose countless other non-Western idioms. Ocularcentrism led to quantitative approaches to knowledge and to principles of "scientific objectivity," which for many commentators (e.g., Cosgrove, 2008; Warf, 2008) had dramatic consequences. At the epistemological level, researchers remained unaware of their own subjectivities; at the ontological one, their reliance on linear time, Euclidian space, and sight as the most trustworthy of the senses had critical and material impacts on human lives.

Ontologically naïve and epistemologically flawed, the civilising and interpreting missions of anthropology were in crisis. Clifford Geertz initiated a philological turn influenced by French thinkers (Paul Ricoeur, Michel Foucault, Gilles Deleuze, Jacques Derrida) and Russian literary critic Mikhail Bakhtin. To be sure, postmodern doubts about what qualifies as knowledge (Lyotard, 1979) gave the discipline a literary flavour and a new impetus organised around the politics and ethics of authority (authorless, dialogical, or polyphonic texts), the poetics of representation (evocations, fictions, and the partial truths or carnivalesque arenas of heteroglossia), but also the experiences and emotions of the field. Postmodern anthropology is in this context inclined to Sophism—for Protagoras "everything" was true. As Jameson (1983: 114), Bourdieu (1993: 9–10), or Clifford and Marcus (1986: 2) point out, William Faulkner, James Joyce, Ernest Hemingway, or Virginia Woolf abandoned omniscient narration in favour of a plurality of coexisting (and sometimes competing) perspectives. Centuries before, Miguel de Cervantes gave different names to the same characters in *Don Quixote*, and also played with various registers in order to reconstruct the polyvalence words have for different minds.

The popularity and media coverage of anthropology faltered around the same period (1970s). Academic jobs and budgets were cut. The postmodern legacy, together with increased career pressures and shorter fieldwork periods, gradually translated into novel research practices and experimental writing styles. Thus anthropology "at home" (Jackson, 1987) and multi-sited ethnography (Marcus, 1995, 1998) leave passé quests for exoticism behind, and the anthropology of globalisation (Bamford and Robbins, 1997; Inda and Rosaldo, 2002) or "cosmopolitan" ethnography (Appadurai, 1996: 49–52) get to grips with the complexities of today's worldwide interactions. Fieldwork hops from one location to another, follows people's trajectories, and must accept the impossibility of staying with these people for extensive periods of time. Caught up in the hectic pace of survival, job hunting, and so forth, people have little time to spare an anthropologist unless they draw immediate benefit from her presence (Hours and Selim, 2010: 215). Ambitious methodological directions were designed in such challenging contexts. For example, critical ethnography (Thomas, 1992; Madison, 2011) is concerned with the ethics of research practices as explored in feminist, queer, and postcolonial theories. At the textual level, such practices give birth to subtle writing strategies. Gorzelsky (2004: 75) cites the writings of Fox (1996) and Fischer and Abedi (1990), to whom we could add Crapanzano (2004), Stewart (2007), Myerhoff (1974), and many others driven by models of "dialogical" or "collaborative" ethnographies, which promote multivocality and blur the distinction between researchers and participants (Dwyer, 1977; Rabinow, 1977; Lacoste-Dujardin, 1977; Dumont, 1991; Shostak, 2000; Lassiter, 2001, 2005; Kral and Idlout, 2006: 55; Robben and Sluka, 2007: 21).

No culture

No authenticity

The anthropology of globalisation articulates the local and the global through an inescapable convergence and homogenisation. As human differences disintegrate with the circulation of people, information, and capital across borders, the concept of an authentic and spatialised "culture" has lost much of its significance and therefore relevance for anthropology. A number of anthropologists even associate this spatialised concept to the nationalist influence of Western anthropological thought (Bhabha, 1989: 64; Hastrup and Olwig, 1997: 4). Today's "field," in reality, is everywhere and nowhere; it is placeless (Killick, 1995: 104; Okely, 1996: 3; Caputo, 2000: 27; Pink, 2000: 99; Norman, 2000: 120; Robben and Sluka, 2007: 25). In a mobile world of diaspora and mass movements of populations, space and identities are reterritorialised, familiar lines between "here" and "there" blurred (Gupta and Ferguson, 1992; Searles, 2006: 90).

Claude Lévi-Strauss' (1955) pessimistic and oddly compelling vision in *Tristes Tropiques* deplored the disappearance of diversity, of exoticism, of the elsewhere in our increasingly homogenised and banalised world. Arthur de Gobineau, Pierre Loti, and Maurice Barrès had mourned the same loss before him; so had Henri Michaux (1968: 35), complaining in 1929 that our world, now that humanity travelled around it, is "rinsed of its exoticism" and there is nothing left to us. More recent tourism studies echo the same concerns. The freedom to travel is dying out insofar as people can only see what they are shown. The world has become a touristic stage, a scenic design of culture. Fashions, rites, and performances are "pseudo-events" (Boorstin, 2012), "hyperreal" simulations (Eco, 1995; Baudrillard, 1981) maintained for sightseers. Tourism, which has been seen as a quest for authenticity and for the self (MacCannell, 1999), is in perpetual conflict with the fake. In ethnic tourism, the natives put on a show of folklore, of "phony-folk-culture" (Forster, 1964: 226; van den Berghe and Keys, 1984). MacCannell (1992: 18, 168, 170) refers to "reconstructed ethnicity"—in his words, "many formerly primitive groups earn their living by charging visitors admission to their sacred shrines, ritual performances, and displays of more or less 'ethnologized' everyday life." Ethnic tourism therefore represents "the mirror image of racism." Thus in Mali, the Dogons instrumentalise tourists just as they are instrumentalised, for example, selecting salient features described in the works of Marcel Griaule and amplifying them. Such fabrications of ethnicity, or "indigenous ethnology," existed prior to mass tourism—at a colonial exhibition in 1907, a group of Chaamba paraded as Touaregs (Cauvin-Verner, 2007: 112, 141).

What is anthropology for?

Accordingly, there have been various attempts to salvage "dying" cultures. Barbara Myerhoff (1974: 25) wanted to salvage the rituals of an endangered people, to tell their story "as they told it to me, so that it shall not be forgotten." Victor Turner (1975: 40) was allowed to publish a full account of Ndembu rituals because the adepts "were aware that it would not be long before most of [these rituals] would be forgotten by the young people." The writings of Franz Boas like recent accounts outside anthropology (e.g., Kerr, 1996) strive to write cultures and sustain them before they disappear forever. These attempts indicate that the meaning of culture has shifted (like marriage and all things cultural) and become unrecognisable from what it used to be. Today, they also create more problems than they solve. Referring human life to culture is no more edifying, in Michael Jackson's (2005: xii) opinion, than reducing it to nature. The nature/culture dualism does not even make sense for Maurice Merleau-Ponty (1945: 220–221), who notes with reference to Malinowski's *Father in Primitive Psychology* that all our behaviours derive from nature and at the same time escape the simplicity of animal life—everything in us is biological, and everything is cultural too. Why should we assume that subjects will enunciate this thing called culture? When culture is reduced to showcases, when it is negotiated only in festivals, it publicly accepts its reification. It displays stuffed people in a Museum of Natural History and makes of the world a ghost village more than a global village. "Reconstructed ethnicity," MacCannell (1992: 168) contends, uses "former colourful ways both as commodities to be bought and sold, and as rhetorical weaponry in their dealings with one another." Anthropological wisdom would probably consist, for Hours and Selim (2010: 158–159), in acknowledging the mortality of cultures (just like that of people). "What if," Paul Rabinow (2008: 54) ventures, "we did not begin with the assumption that our task was to write culture?"

A corollary of this ailing concept of culture is that the great divide between an allegedly homogeneous "West" and an equally homogeneous "East" are flawed constructions (Said, 1978; Huizer and Mannheim, 1979), along with other generic categorisations of people ("the Nuer," "the Balinese," "the English," "the Japanese," and so forth). They oversimplify the complexity of human relations and disrespect their diversity; they exoticise or even offend communities; and far too much is lost in translation. For example, anthropological studies of the same village or the same society have produced radically different results (Stoller, 1989: 144). If the written text is determined by the contingencies and serendipities of a relationship, that between *one* anthropologist (who could have been someone else) and *some* informants (who could all have been different), then the "knowledge" that this text produces may be distinct from, but not more reliable than tourist guides, cultural stereotypes, and political diatribes. Moving away from Malinowski's canon of fieldwork as "far away" and "timeless" towards the study of the contemporary, the here-and-now, anthropologists therefore "experience profound temporal turbulences precisely because they can no longer make assumptions about what is necessary for their method to produce rich ethnographic data" (Rabinow and Marcus, 2008: 7). So, what is anthropology today? What to do with culture? And to what extent is it possible for social sciences to think outside taxonomies? Bowker and Leigh Star (2000: 1, 3) remark that categories in anthropology have been "clues to the core organizing principles for colonial western understandings of 'primitive' culture," conceding at the same time that "to classify is human." If today there is no West, no East, no White, no Native, no subject, and no object, and in the end no culture, perhaps there is no-thing on which anthropology may have a credible discourse. The discipline loses its object, along with possibilities of generalisation. But rather than focusing on the past (history) and present (locality) of "culture," anthropology's current trend, as reported in Borneman and Hammoudi's (2009: 4) thought-provoking book, is to imagine *futures*.

Subjectivity-based guilt

Reflexivity

This interest in futures, tackled in a later section, is a direct consequence of the postmodern crisis. And I would like to suggest that anthropology has not yet recovered from this crisis, whose magnitude in the 1980s opened a methodological Pandora's box. What anthropologists deem worth knowing, for example, still differs from one country to another (Ribeiro and Escobar, 2008). Also, issues of identity and subjectivity embedded in the postmodern effort are still at stake. Works on identity are clearly dominant in the titles and subtitles of monographs published from the late 1980s onwards (Rabinow and Marcus, 2008: 34). They raise awareness of the impacts of social processes on fieldwork, or what researchers call "reflexivity" (Marcus, 1998: 189–201; Denzin and Lincoln, 2003: 283; Aunger, 2004; Alsup, 2004; Etherington, 2004; Hammersley and Atkinson, 2007: 14–18). Reflexivity is a polemical and slippery concept through which anthropologists ponder how their practices interfere in other people's relationships and distort their "data"; in other words, how their presence shapes the field. Observers disrupt, especially over long or repeated periods of time, the lifestyles of the observed. Their very research modifies, in the ironic twists of the Hawthorne effect, the subjects of their research. Thus the ethnographic expeditions of Marcel Griaule in Mali, and the touristic reputation that ensued, shaped the ways in which the Dogons see themselves. Anthropology in arctic regions has transformed the tundra and the Inuit who, reacting to their new identities as objects of investigation, crafted emblematic traits of their culture that reinforce contrasts between Inuit and *qalunaat* worlds (Searles, 2006; Wachowich, 2006: 127). Identities in this way adjust and mutate. Anthropologists and informants *change each other*, which makes their relationship (e.g., between colonisers and colonised in classic ethnographies, as read by Renalto Rosaldo and Michael Taussig) extremely difficult to understand (McKenzie Stevens, 2004: 166–167). Reflexivity recognises that fieldwork is relational—it is not the world of others, but occurs between myself and others. To be reflexive is therefore to make my past experience available to myself and others, to represent memory, to make it *present* (Fabian, 1983: 91). James Clifford (1988: 14, 152) expresses the same concept of relation when he cites Segalen, for whom the ethnographer must express "not simply his vision, but through an instantaneous, constant *transfer*, the echo of his presence."

Building on this reflexive intuition, Michel Leiris (1973, 1976, 1988) incorporates his own reactions to the field and writes his existence through people. He composes surrealist *journaux intimes*, unconventional autobiographies that mix genres. Dreams play a remarkable role in *Phantom Africa*, where he notes that "the real subject of the journal is the ethnography of the ethnographer" (Hand, 2004: 57). Jérôme Becker was already concluding in 1887 that "everything is matter for personal exploration on this mysterious Continent [Africa]" (Fabian, 2000: 92). The hybrid writings of Segalen and Leiris recall amalgams between the

Japanese I-novel (*watakushi shōsetsu*) and the autobiographical forms it both borrows and differentiates itself from (Lippit, 2001: 204–205). Like the I-novel in the 1910s and 1920s, the surrealist imprint on the anthropology of the 1930s and 1940s might as well build on the idea that "the basis of all art lies in the self [*watakushi*]" (Kume Masao, cited in Suzuki, 1996: 51). Keeping to the tradition of Leiris' work, books by Paul Rabinow (1977), Jean-Paul Dumont (1991), Vincent Crapanzano (1980), or Jeanne Favret-Saada (1980) are frequently cited as classical texts of reflexivity. Most anthropologists today would regard autobiography as part of their records (Fetterman, 1989: 45; Brewer, 2000: 59; Creighton, 2007: 414). Some, like Barbara Myerhoff (1974), Renato Rosaldo (1993), or Ruth Behar (1996), suggest that ethnographers embrace the emotive power of autobiography. Others choose to focus on their own sexuality (Kulick and Willson, 1995; Markowitz and Ashkenazi, 1999), or even take reality as a cue rather than a purpose and move to fiction—thus Laura Bohannan's pen name (Bowen, 1954) gives her freedom to express her self, in a novel that draws on her fieldwork in West Africa.

The headache of the "I"

There is a great philosophical tradition of first-person writing, manifest in the works of Saint Augustine, Descartes, Rousseau, or Wittgenstein. Philosophy is "work on oneself" for Wittgenstein, who also exclaims in his *Notebooks*: "The I, the I, is what is deeply mysterious!" The philosophical "I" may refer to a collective and rather impersonal human condition, or simply *me* as opposed to everyone else. And for Pihlström (2011: 109–110) *my* writing should confess my own guilt, not someone else's or that of human beings in general. Likewise and as suggested above, anthropology is "inherently autobiographic" (Fabian, 1983: 87), hence there is a sense in which "all social science is autobiographical" (Agar, 1980: 42). Knowledge about others begins with the self—this observation is sure to give writers a headache. For the anthropologist's notebook can be seen as a methodologically archaic and naïve mode of inscription, attached to the Western sensibility of selfhood, to the Cartesian "I" according to which "seeing is believing" (Comaroff and Comaroff, 1992: 8, 25–26). My challenge lies in the fact that autobiography *lies*—in philosophy and literature, the diaries of Saint Augustine, Michel de Montaigne, Jean-Jacques Rousseau, Leo Tolstoy, Marcel Proust, Jean-Paul Sartre, James Joyce, Romain Gary, and countless others are not clearly separated from fiction. When Roland Barthes (1970) writes Japan, he is aware that among all erudite discourses the ethnographic type is the closest to fiction; he knows that his representations, however astute they have appeared to my eyes, are mythologies (Martin, 1996: 23). Likewise, ethnography as *fiction* (Geertz, 1973: 15; Clifford and Marcus, 1986) or "creative nonfiction" (Agar, 1995) deceives, and in such circumstances reflexivity is likely to degenerate into narcissism or navel-gazing (Perry, 1989: 6; Killick, 1995: 102; Silverman, 1997: 239–240; Colic-Peisker, 2004: 91; Robinson, 2004: 164; Aunger, 2004: 9, 11; Horner, 2004: 29; Alsup, 2004: 221), despite claims to the contrary (Okely and Callaway, 1992: xi, 2; Taussig, 1992: 45).

So how much reflexivity is required to understand the research context (Horner, 2004: 29)? Suggesting that self-discovery is "not to be pushed too far," Van Maanen (1995: 29) vaguely answers that the limits of reflexivity are "a most open question." Others (Gallop, Brandt, Herrington *inter alia*) consider that extreme reflexivity has backfired and distanced researchers from their participants (Alsup, 2004: 222). Weary of ethnographic analysis, anthropologists prefer to hear about other anthropologists and teach students about them rather than anthropology (Ben-Ari, 1995: 131). Marshall Sahlin's anecdote, reported by Marcus and subsequently Van Maanen (1995: 29), is in this regard very telling: "But as the Fijian said to the New Ethnographer, 'That's enough talking about you, let's talk about me!'" Psychoanalyst Wilfred Bion (in Ciccone and Ferrant, 2009: 112) used to contend in the same vein that analysis tells us more about the analyst than about the patient. In any case, there is no final answer to deciding about an adequate level of author's biography, nor even to introducing the voices of others as if they had chosen *this* text to speak for themselves. There is no ideal way of representing the fieldwork experience (Stewart, 1996: 210). And what counts, to begin with, as "experience"? In what ways and to what ends are we to represent it (Schroeder, 2004: 55)? Postmodern ethnographers like to alternate between evocations and exegeses, between one literary genre and another. Whether ethnography can achieve analytical rigour along a poetic and introspective path is a matter of debate. Even the I-novel, despite the transparency of its fictional status, received criticisms that were strictly identical to those against reflexivity in anthropology. The I-novel was "too narrowly concerned with the private agonies of its authors, and too little aware of the feelings of surrounding individuals and ideas" (Gessel and Matsumoto, 1985: ii).

Let us argue at this point that self-absorption is anthropology's *péché mignon* (literally "cute sin," that is, guilty pleasure) or Achilles' heel—a possibly tragic, but not hopeless tendency; a condition requiring constant monitoring, but not necessarily palliative care. The idea that there is something wrong with the "I" is not new; at the same time the "I" appears as a promising direction. In fact, this "don't-but go ahead" logic has produced some of the finest guilt in anthropological writing, which deserves expansion.

Coping with guilt

Strategic confession

As anthropological knowledge originates in often problematic "findings" of the field encounter, the same old issues of experience (fieldwork) and representation (writing) remain: How should one represent the complexity of human relations? For Scheper-Hughes (2000) there is "no 'politically correct' way of doing anthropology." Most researchers invent their method "out of the muddiness of field experience" (Robinson, 2004: 165). As a result, researchers express "anxiety and guilt" about their methods, seen as "unethical," "highly questionable," "dishonest," and so forth (Jackson, 1995: 44, 60). The reason why guilt is so pervasive in anthropological research is hardly mysterious. Any kind of social relation challenges ethics; anthropology is mainly concerned with representing these social relations; and therefore representation can never be ethical enough, encouraging researchers to confess uneasy emotions. I think it is possible to dissect such confessions into an apparatus of methodological transgression. What fascinates me is that the inclusion of the self in anthropology is both the *outcome* of structural guilt and the *cause* of yet again more guilt. In other words guilt produces, in some absurd circle, its own generator. So perhaps the self is less a problematic necessity than a necessary problem, than something we need precisely *because* of the problem it creates. In my view, self-contemplation (excessive reflexivity) cannot represent just an excuse to indulge in stylistic navel-gazing to the detriment of people. Rather, it is a strategic device through which anthropologists endure the guilt they perceive in their methods. Reflexivity is enacted in the rhetoric of justification—my methods are wrong and I have sinned much, but by describing them as necessary evil at least, my peers grant me forgiveness. Of course I feel guilty, how would I not? But at the same time I had no choice, given anthropological knowledge surfaces with transgression, with the sordidness inhabiting us. The early practices of modern medicine were enabled by the "forbidden" dissections of dead bodies. Understanding bodily mechanisms and diseases required a transgression of religious rules preserving the immortality of the soul. As science violates and tears apart, so too does fieldwork. This strategic discourse of the self resembles the apparatus of confession through which Michel Foucault (1994b: 78–90) elucidates sexuality in Western societies. Power neither concealed nor censored sex; on the contrary it led people to reveal their practices, to tell themselves. Are ethnographers not led, in the same way, to disclose the mediocrity of their methods, to confide in their clan, to plead guilty? I only want to detail below such creative uses of guilt.

Managing shame

Because tourists (and increasingly anthropologists) do not have much time to spare, they sometimes prefer non-humans to humans, photographs to language. As Tzvetan Todorov (1992: 453) puts it, "Seeing camels is less dangerous than seeing people." It is far less stressful to avoid encounters with other people, who could call our identity into question. But there is something shameful in focusing on your camera rather than on indigenous populations. Michel (2004: 56–61) notes that tourists are ashamed of seeing themselves in the mirror of the other tourist (the tourist is always the other), and at the same time have no problem practising the tourism they castigate, as soon as they get holidays. This contempt that tourists have for themselves represents a form of racism opposing tourists to a rigid ideal-type of the Great Explorer. I sense that the same interplay between fear of the other (xenophobia) and a certain fear of oneself (shame) structures anthropology. Michel (2004: 155) cites anthropologist Dibie, who after making so many friends around the world and seeing "the bizarre, the comic, the strange," cannot imagine how "one might be scared of anyone else than oneself." Lacanian psychoanalysis throws light on this existential interlocking where angst and shame mingle (e.g., Lacan, 2004); so does literature, in the works of Edgar Allan Poe and Guy de Maupassant's short story *Fear*, for example. Oppressed by the guilt of her affair, Irene wonders in Stefan Zweig's *Fear*:

Do you think it's... it's always just fear that... that keeps people from speaking out? Couldn't it be... well, couldn't it be shame? Suppose they're ashamed to talk about it and expose themselves in front of so many people?

Anthropologists do write their shame of opening their heart, of being who they are, of being self-conscious, of desiring, of existing. And embarrassed about autobiography, they feel the need to legitimise it. Often they identify the origins of shame in their debatable presence and role among their community of adoption, and inscribe them in expressions of discomfort and shyness. Thus Morton (1995: 170) felt "quite uncomfortable about that attraction [to Tongan men], with its possible overtones of racism." Forsey's (2004: 59) friend understood his "discomfort" at being labelled a spy. A lot of Hine's (2001: 66) time was spent "rather uncomfortably hanging out, trying to look as though [she] was doing something." Birckhead (2004: 99) tells us about his "youth, basic shyness, and lack of confidence as a fieldworker." Inside her Mexican brothel Kelly (2004: 6, 16) was "somewhat shy at first" and her fieldwork "often messy" and "awkward." Rethmann (2007: 50–51) had to let go of her "discomfiture," of her "shame," and of "the stories [she] was telling [herself] about [herself]." Rabinow's (1977: 79) "gestures were wrong, [his] language was off, [his] questions were strange, and interpersonal malaise was all too frequently the dominant mood."

Typical accounts open with the anthropologist's ignorance and faux-pas, even if before long she sees the light, dissipates confusions, and displays confident knowledge. At first then, the anthropologist "makes a fool of herself" (Kenna, 1992: 148). Faced with people who question her knowledge and behaviour, she also tries not to lose face (and if you pardon the pun, not to lose faith). When a native tells Chagnon (1974: 35) that as a foreigner he should know how canoes are made, for example, the anthropologist retorts that "he [knows] how to make them (which was not exactly true) but [he] [does] not have the appropriate tools with which to do it." In her account of the Lesu on the island of New Ireland (Melanesia) in 1929–1930, Powdermaker (1967: 108–109) expresses shame as episodic impossibilities to maintain a distance. After repeatedly declining to join the dancing rites, the Western anthropologist, the specialist of culture, gives in:

> Consumed with self-consciousness, I imagined my family and friends sitting in the background and muttering in disapproving tone, "Hortense,

dancing with the savages!" How could I get up before all these people of the Stone Age and dance with them?

Jean Briggs' (1970: 20) fieldwork among the Utkus reports the same kind of shame as loss of distance. The Eskimo lifestyle had for her a romantic appeal "since early childhood" and she secretly hoped that she "might discover [herself] essentially Eskimo at heart." In her own words she

> voiced no such romanticism aloud, however. I was rather ashamed of my "unprofessional" attitude; and I had a number of qualms concerning the wisdom of being adopted, in terms of loss of "objective" position in the community.

In both cases, shame is clearly caused by the fear of losing one's status of "intellectual" (and therefore superior to the "non-intellectuals" studied).

Not only are anthropologists likely to be ashamed of their predecessors, they also fear that posterity might see comparable mistakes in what they do. Many researchers consequently introduce the reflexive device, whose therapeutic function alleviates shame. This self-treatment has a sacred dimension insofar as it may resort to self-punishment, to the masochist repentance of the sinner. For example, Renato Rosaldo (1993: 7) "hesitates" about introducing himself into his account, both because the self-absorbed "I" loses sight of the culturally different Other and is therefore taboo, and because this taboo is violated "by essays laced with trendy amalgams of continental philosophy and autobiographical snippets." As an ethnographer however, "[he] must enter the discussion at this point to elucidate certain issues of method." Raymond Firth (2004: 10) did not show more confidence in 1936 when he introduced his study of the Tikopia with a "somewhat egoistic recital (...) because some account of the relations of the anthropologist to his people is relevant to the nature of his results." Vincent Crapanzano (1980: 133) is only engaged in autobiography "in the most tenuous sense" and has no interest in confession and expiation, "though both confession and expiation enter inevitably into [his] enterprise." Michael Taussig (1992: 45) has a conventional understanding of reflexivity as a "procedure of contextualisation" that admits his presence and "enormously confused understandings of history"; however, such contextualisation is neither autobiography nor narcissism for him, because "it opens up to a science of mediations—neither Self nor Other but their mutual co-implicatedness." Kathleen Stewart (2007: 5) does away with the "I" altogether, calling herself "she" to distinguish "between this writerly identity and the kind of subject that arises as a daydream of simple presence." "She" senses and imagines, not truth, but "some possibilities."

In this way much anthropological writing reveals its own weakness in order to conceal, in a rather cowardly and perverse fashion, the weaknesses of the human heart; and I cannot but love-and-hate the *ingenuous* religiosity embedded in such *ingenious* writing tricks. Confessions range from the passing apology to the utmost despair and, when explicit enough, mainly originate from the author's appreciation of her own *integration* as unethical. By integration I mean the successful achievement of reciprocal acceptance and respect, a situation of "cultural intimacy" (Herzfeld, 1997), whereby both researcher and researched feel comfortable with each other. How do anthropologists understand, not just the process but the conditions of integration? The next section argues that integration in the field routinely fails, either because it "lacks" or because it is so "overwhelming" that it cannot be appropriately dealt with. Lacks and excesses of integration may even strangely coexist.

No integration: the "lacks"

Boredom and exasperations

Fieldwork is emotionally straining. When Lévi-Strauss (1955: 227) stayed with the Bororo, who dedicated the nights to religious chants and rested during the day, he was sometimes "too exhausted to be a good ethnographer." Birckhead (2004: 98) "agonized over [his] role as observer." There were "many difficult moments" when Rethmann (2007: 51) "hated fieldwork," moments she associated with failure. Having spent nineteen months in her Botswanan field where she "wanted immediate rapport, immediate understanding, immediate confidences" with !Kung women, Marjorie Shostak (2000: 32–33) was losing her patience (and possibly her temper):

> The strain of having been away from home so long, the continual pressure of adapting to other people's ways, the hard work of collecting reliable information about their lives, and the demands of the physical environment had exhausted me.

It could have been much worse.

Alfred Métraux's letter to Rivière from Easter Island does not beat about the bush in 1934: "I have a horror of the inhabitants of this island: it is difficult to imagine a population more vilely degenerated" (Rivière, 2010: 163). Hearing dreadful news about a local ruler, Jérôme Becker writes in the 1880s: "What a dark wasp's nest this Africa is, always at war, always hungry for murder and looting, and where man's ferocity goes to battle with the hostility of the soil and the climate!" (Fabian, 2000: 63). Michel Leiris' (1988: 111) irritation speaks volumes about colonial relationships:

> Seeing how impatient I am with the blacks who get on my nerves, I realise the degree of bestiality reached by those who, in their relations with the natives, are exhausted by the climate and free from any ideology... And what must it be like among the Berger [anise-flavoured liqueur] and whiskey enthusiasts!

Leaving France with the excitements and hopes of exotic adventures, Leiris is increasingly disillusioned by the reality of hostile weather conditions, insipid foods, loneliness, and the brutishness of colonial bureaucracy (see also Hand, 2004: 56). Malinowski's diary (1967: 144, 188) contains the same frustrations and impressions of indecency. He feels "a bit vulgar" and heads back home when the villagers of Tukwa'ukwa roar with laughter, entertained by the jokes of a man "saying indecent things." Every so often the field is irremediably boring, or full of irritating individuals. Böhm, during the German East African expedition in the 1880s, felt "bored in this place to the point of losing [his] mind (...)" (Fabian, 2000: 182). Malinowski (1922: 3) writes his experience in strikingly similar terms, explaining that his boredom is rooted in a lack of connection with people. He remembers "the feeling of hopelessness and despair after many obstinate but futile attempts had entirely failed to bring [him] into real touch with the natives."

Self-control

Political correctness understates, in writing, the violence of real encounters. It is difficult to picture, for instance, what Muir (2004: 196) really means when he admits that he "did not much like" a field he characterises as "fraught." The embellishments of scientific or literary pride only hint at obnoxious behaviours. After three years in the field, where Chagnon (1974: 163) had to endure "the contempt that the native people have for [anthropologists]," his patience began to "wear very thin." Self-control became an issue. He "felt irresistible compulsions to lay aside [his] professionalism and responsibilities as a 'dispassionate observer' and give free rein to [his] passions." Remembering his dislike mixed with jealousy towards a certain Möawä, Chagnon (1974: 196) concludes with candour that "scientific curiosity brought [him] to this village and professional obligation kept [him] there in circumstances [he] did not particularly enjoy." Perry's (1989: 21) fieldwork in Lesotho consisted of "claustrophobic involvement with other people" which made him "lose [his] temper and sulk when events conspired (as [he] thought) to thwart [him]." He found it difficult, in other words, to "control mood swings." In such passages the reader realises at once that anthropologists report what they want, and hide the rest. Trusting their account implies accepting the role of fiction and deception in anthropological representation.

Attempting to control or channel their emotions, fieldworkers find themselves "unnaturally" distant—they observe incompatibilities between their work and normal human reactions. Yet even *they* are not immune to apprehensions, fears of others (literally xenophobia), and all sorts of rejections that could precipitate their discipline into disrepute. Resisting the urge to interfere in the lives of informants, for Vincent Crapanzano (1972: 19, 22), calls for "a degree of restraint which can impose severe strains on [the anthropologist's] usual way of managing his emotional life." He felt "a sort of emotional deprivation" among Native Americans, due to the same experience of excessive detachment he describes in Morocco (Crapanzano, 1980: 135): looking back over his field notes, he is "immediately struck by the impoverished quality of [his] emotional response. [His] questions seem frequently cold, unemotional, and detached."

Solitude

Long after fieldwork, frustrations remain vivid, as if the people encountered returned as mares oppressing researchers. Mulcock avoided looking at her field notes for almost three years, as "the thought of reliving many of the experiences and apparent failures of that time was simply too hard to face" (Hume and Mulcock, 2004: xiv). "No matter how often we enter an Inuit household for the first time," Lee's (2006: 25) field notes read, "it never loses its terror for me." Hence anthropologists seek to disconnect themselves from the reality they threw themselves in. They allow their minds and bodies to wander off *elsewhere*. Reading fiction and writing to friends and relatives enable a mental escape; physical exercise and voluntary isolation respectively shut off and divert thinking. Crick (1992: 186) spent "much time reading novels, being bored, hating the place [he] was in, and having very mixed feelings about the people [he] was with." Malinowski (1922: 3) had "periods of despondency, when [he] buried [himself] in the reading of novels, as a man might take to drink in a fit of tropical depression and boredom." To escape from this "pandemonium" of irritating niggers, in which he "[suffered] horribly," he found solace in gymnastics—"a time of concentration and solitude." His *boys* and a certain "Ginger" got so much on his nerves that he "[understood] all the German and Belgian colonial atrocities" (Malinowski, 1967: 276, 279). Margaret Mead confessed in her private letters that she was homesick, lonely, frustrated, and that she "[could] eat native food, but (...) [couldn't] live on it for six months" (Shankman, 2009: 90–91).

In Shostak's (2000: 26, 33) case, dread towards Nisa's unrequired company and verbosity "soon turned to dislike, first mild, then stronger," and the anthropologist "felt she needed a place to go where [she] could close [her] ears and eyes, where [she] could stop hearing and stop responding." In her loneliness, she "no longer felt capable of exerting the necessary effort to gain acceptance," and was ready to be "where [she] could be alone when [she] wanted to, for hours at a time, undisturbed by requests from anyone." Likewise, Evans-Pritchard's (1940: 14–15) tent was literally invaded by "tireless visitors" who, albeit providing opportunities for practising the Nuer language, imposed a "severe strain" on the anthropologist. Nevertheless he "became hardened, though never entirely insensitive, to performing the most intimate operations before an audience"; and the intimacy he was forced to establish with the Nuer compensated for the loss of privacy and occasions for confidential conversations. When an informant asked Michael Taussig (1992: 34) if he could stay in his apartment in his absence, the author

> felt the most terrible coward, especially because my cowardice took the form of not being able to tell him that I thought his situation was too dangerous, for that would tear open the facade of normalcy that I at least felt we so badly needed.

Anthropologists like most people dislike the systematic sharing of what they have and what they feel. Morton (1995: 172) faced "a complete lack of privacy (...) and resentment at having to 'share' all [her] belongings and income." Jean Briggs (1970: 20) was very similarly worried about "drains on [her] supplies which would result from contributing to the maintenance of a family household; and loss of privacy with resultant difficulties in working." Briggs (1970: 27–28) and her Inuits ended up avoiding each other. The Inuits' "unfailing anticipation of [her] needs" aroused her

> guilt concerning the one need that would never occur to them: my desire for solitude. (...) I could not help seeing them also as an invasion of privacy. I felt trapped by my visitors. (...) Six days passed before I escaped. (...) I fled to the tundra and wandered there all day, memorizing Eskimo words and feeling homesick. It was when I came back into camp late that afternoon that I first realized how important to me my Eskimo neighbours were and how dependent I was on the warmth of their acceptance.

It is also clear later in the text that these people were shocked by her sudden and unexplained disappearance. Just like Shostak, Briggs wants to be alone, and her own fieldwork is a noteworthy repetition of Malinowski's (1922: 5), who used to "go for a solitary walk for an hour or so, return again and then quite naturally seek out the natives' society, this time as a relief from loneliness."

So the impossibility to live with people, coupled with an impossibility to live away from them, produces the shame of not being able to eschew the so-called herd instinct. Integration is so ambiguous a phenomenon that solitude might be "shared" with an informant, and result in an odd mixture of integration and exclusion. It is for example ironic that Paul Rabinow (1977: 68), after viewing the attitude of his first informant as colonial, does not seem to behave differently. Asked whether he would like to sleep with one of the girls, he answers that he will "go with the third woman who had joined [them] for dinner. She had her own room next door, so we could have our privacy." Later he experiences this very classic "invasion of privacy" described above (Rabinow, 1977: 113–114):

> I reassured an edgy Malik that everything was okay, not to worry, but I just wanted to be alone. I started to walk off in the direction of some outlying fields, and Malik followed. The Moroccans never really understood why anyone would want to take a walk by himself. I remembered my scene with Ali at the wedding (...) I was tired and wanted to be by myself. I would see him the following day. A look of dismay and hurt crossed his face. He said, wash sekren?—are you drunk?

Feeling dizzy as if "on the edge of an abyss," the anthropologist concludes that "a vast gulf lay between us and could never be bridged." In other words, we are different and that's that. The natives might do what they want, so do anthropologists. When communication fails, it just fails.

Years later in Morocco again, Cauvin-Verner (2007: 207) expresses mixed feelings about local reactions to her needs for isolation:

> After ten years of research, I still have to overcome the challenge of their deliberate lies, as if I was going to divulge the secrets everyone was informed about. (...) I do not always surrender to the moral of my hosts. For example I often go for a walk, on my own. They do not stop me but it obviously creates problems. Women fear that something might happen to me (...) I do not give reasons for my jaunts into European hotels where I have my beer. I do not boast about it either. But I know that rumours spread fast across town.

Perhaps this confession is a politically correct version of what she really felt. And how can the reader know, without asking her?

Apart from the occasional reflexive passages such as the above, relatively few anthropologists are willing to publish their failures of long-term integration (Muir, 2004: 185, 198); and when they do, more often than not they turn these failures into successes. For example, losing a friend is also a professional victory for Hendry (1992: 170), who "at the cost of a good relationship" deepens her understanding of the subject and therefore identifies the same productivity in her mistakes as in Briggs' (1970). Hume and Mulcock's (2004: xii) collection seeks to "highlight the potential productivity of such ethnographic discomfort and awkwardness." Thus Hume's (Hume and Mulcock, 2004: xiii) unwelcome presence "gave [her] deep insight into life at Yarrabah"; fieldwork is for Kelly (2004: 16) "like sex, even bad sex, (...) always productive: it produces sensations, emotions, intimate knowledge of oneself and others"; following the traditional phase of awkwardness, Birckhead (2004: 99) persists, "to be rewarded by deeper access to the saints and their world." Oftentimes methodological failure fuels an unconscious pleasure and pride of being rejected, which makes the anthropologist special. Stoller (1989: 4–5, 121, 125) delights in his hurdles like so many opportunities to point out he could overcome them and learn from them. His first month of fieldwork was a "total failure" because "most Songhay refused to cooperate with [him]." And yet—he "had the temerity to ask strange questions" and made "friends who were impressed by [his] command of the Songhay language" and "liked [him] a lot"; his temerity also extended to "the comforts of a world in which we are members of an intellectual elite and enter worlds of experience in which our illiterate teachers scold us for our ignorance." His adventure is not dissimilar to Evans-Pritchard's (1940: 10–15), who for a long period was ostracised by the Nuer; but despite their "obstinate resistance" and serious health problems that affected his expeditions, the anthropologist became "more friendly" with them, to the point of being "compelled to be a member" of the community.

No description

The superficiality of integration translates not just in methodologically unsound, but also disappointing texts. Even classic figures such as Malinowski, Gluckman, Turner, Lévi-Strauss, Fortes, Geertz, and others, Michael Jackson (2005: xxvi) deplores, use selected details to justify an interpretation, thereby failing to describe an event "so fully or entirely that we, the readers, may see for ourselves the wealth of meanings it contains." For Biehl, Good, and Kleinman (2007: 14), anthropology's overemphasis on cultural representation has downplayed the significance of lived experience: "For a discipline that focuses on 'experience-near' analyses, the conceptualization of experience is by and large very thin." Participant observation, Jack Goody (2010: 59) acknowledges, allows only sporadic scribbles that will be used as memorandum to reconstruct the day's happenings. With only pencils and paper, he was incapable of using musical notation to record the music of the LoDagaa, and recomposed prayers from memory, outside their context. Sometimes he would ask an informant to tell him about some event, and wrote directly what she said in his notebook. This general lack of description is easily noticeable in ethnographic studies of organisations (e.g., Miller, 1997; Lien, 1997; Moeran, 1996), which often boil down to conceptual arguments backed up by a few real-life episodes. Parallels are drawn between these episodes and a theoretical literature in a deductive logic of verification, not through a serious compilation of material and inductive process of discovery. In other words, informants' voices become illustrative labels put on theories that were formulated in different contexts. Thus Moeran (1996) spends quite some time in a Japanese advertising agency, but recounts very few events. In another Caribbean agency Miller (1997: 161) admits he saw "snippets, for example the beginnings and ends of campaigns, rather than seeing many all the way through." In sum, as Borneman and Hammoudi (2009: 16) convincingly put it, most ethnographers are guilty of "textualism," of an overreliance on texts—they "prefer philosophical reflection on the practices of textual reading, deconstruction, genealogy of concepts, and discourse analysis to the fieldwork encounter." Borneman and Hammoudi call such philosophical reflection "puppeteering," or "the staging of dialogues between past and present, between theorists, or between theorists and native interlocutors—instead of grappling with the actual dialogues that go on in the field." Fieldworkers, as already hinted above, are not always very fond of the field.

The anxieties of field research result from frustrating failures to establish rapport with people, which intensify anxieties, which erode rapport, and so forth in a vicious circle. The true irony of fieldwork, therefore, is that while anthropologists rightly complain that there is *not enough* integration, they experience at the same time *too much* of it. They want to know people, yet find out in the field that they cannot stand them, and must flee from such recalcitrant objects of study. Exasperated anthropologists may also misbehave and become burdens. And the resulting ethnographies may deliver "too much" text if they do not contain "enough" description. Knowledge from the field, Josephides (1997: 27) observes, is "both partial and excessive." It is to this confusing facet of ethnographic research that I must turn now.

No integration: the "excesses"

Intrusions

To what extent can a stranger integrate a community, and what exactly is meant by "integration"? Most anthropologists will not cope so well in challenging circumstances, and will not readily relinquish their comfort and habits. Neither Bronislaw Malinowski nor Margaret Mead goes native. They do not regard integration as essential, and do not lament their inability to participate in people's lifestyle. What Malinowski (1922: 6) perceives as tolerance is enough for him:

> As the natives saw me constantly every day, they ceased to be interested or alarmed, or made self-conscious by my presence, and I ceased to be a disturbing element in the tribal life which I was to study, altering it by my very approach.

Margaret Mead's plan (quoted in Shankman, 2009: 89), clearly, is to study the Samoans without staying with them. In a letter to Boas, she writes that getting a house of her own is unfortunately impossible, while the advantages of living with a Samoan family would be more than offset by the loss of efficiency due to the food and the nervewracking conditions of living with half a dozen people in the same room, in a house without walls, always sitting on the floor and sleeping in constant expectation of having a pig or a chicken thrust itself upon one's notice.

Hortense Powdermaker (1967: 118) manages to overcome her shame of dancing with the savages of her Melanesian "Stone-Age society," but never fools herself that she has gone native. She "was never truly a part of their lives." Lee (2006: 25) is "poised to insert [herself] uninvited into an Inuit household for purposes other than social." Gerald Berreman's (1972: xxvii–xxviii) presence in a Himalayan village was not desired but "tolerated with considerable indulgence," and he "refrained from going where [he] was not wanted."

How do researchers deal with their outsider status? The categories of "(amateur) tourist" and "(professional) anthropologist" are rather blurred (Michel, 2004: 65, 71–72). We are all travellers if we travel, and travel-writers whether we compose diaries or blogs, publish in magazines or books. Free to indulge in "hit and run" research (Harvey, 2004: 172), anthropologists readily compare themselves to tourists (Crick, 1992), travelling people (Scheper-Hughes, 2000), explorers (Fabian, 2000: 241), or even spies, secret agents, or unwelcome voyeurs (Denzin, 1997: xix) who play at being members of another culture (Piolat, 2011). Unlike life-long friendships, the short and self-interested stays of anthropological projects always result in artificial, superficial, unsolicited relationships (Dwyer, 1977)—*intrusions* rather than proper integration (Scheper-Hughes, 2000). Intrusions and failed attempts at assimilation give birth to various forms of exploitation involving pretence and play. Professional tourists use informants. They publicise intimate aspects of their lives for their own professional purposes (Dubisch, 1995: 31); and they break promises to keep in touch, letting relationships fade once they have returned to a safe and privileged academic environment and published the book that will establish a reputation (Crick, 1992: 186; Gearing, 1995: 210). With their network and grants and possible self-importance, they can choose to stay in exotic places or close to home when children are young, or why not break away from family life and existing friendships (Knowles, 2000: 58). Are they not part of this culturally hybrid, "new global elite" that knows no borders and everywhere feels at home—the winners of our "liquid" modernity (Bauman, 2005: 29)?

No reciprocity

There is of course something unethical about tourism and anthropology, since only one part of the world is able to visit another. The rich visit the poor. In whatever "field," besides, relationships never feel quite right (unless the research is absolutely covert, which will surely raise ethical issues). When I began fieldwork in 2005, I hesitated before revealing my motives, and did it in a matter-of-fact way. Then the copywriter I would work with introduced me to one of his colleagues: "He's going to work with us. He's a Lévi-Strauss. Writing a thesis about our great profession... So he's here to observe us like animals in cages." The colleague was taken aback of course, and with a wry smile, sneered, "That's promising!" Had I been in her position, I think I would have been even more sarcastic. Who did I think I was? Anthropology, from the outset, called for self-loathing. In 1998 Cauvin-Verner (2007: 25) tells the passenger sitting next to her on the plane that she will write about the tour in which he is about to participate. He frowns and says: "So, I'm going to be an object of study?" I find her reaction, as she reports it at least, condescendingly naïve: "I am disappointed (...) and well determined not to challenge again the discernment of my informants." In other words she turns this episode into an anecdote where it casts doubt on her project, and will in various ways shape it.

The intrusions mentioned earlier show the lack of reciprocity in exchanges (Coffey, 1999: 40; Robben and Sluka, 2007: 9). Too often, anthropologists are "intellectually distant from the people whom they study" and fail to design a collaborative form of research that would be useful to them (Kral and Idlout, 2006: 56). When Paul Rabinow (1977: 78) suggests "rather timidly" that he teach English in the Moroccan village of Sidi Lahcen, for instance, he is aware that an anthropologist is not directly helpful to the community. His offer, unsurprisingly, meets a "polite but tepid response." What purpose does an activity that will not increase sustenance or possessions, or solve technical problems, or cure diseases, fulfil? Who benefits from the research and what are the consequences for participants (Brown and Dobrin, 2004: 4)? If anthropologists and tourists engage in parodies of human relations (Crick, 1992: 185–186) and like "parasites on [their] subjects" exploit indigenous populations, then as O'Neill (2001: 229) asks, "what's in it for them?" "There have been days," Lee (2006: 32) must admit, "when moving around a village with an anthropologist trudging in her wake—someone who is culturally the equivalent of a Yup'ik five-year old—has proven too much for Flora

[Lee's informant]." Flora found it frustrating to have a "clumsy" and "helpless" person along when she wanted to socialise in the steam bath. The "parasite" image fits equally well with Jean Brigg's (1970) behaviour in the Canadian arctic. Finding her double role as participant ("daughter") and observer difficult, she refused to share her belongings and became irritable, disobedient, and overall disrespectful of Inuit culture. The situation deteriorated into a conflict and the group asked her to take her bad temper somewhere else.

To cut a long story short, people suffer from hit and run research. Vine Deloria, Jr. (1973: 134), a Sioux student, harshly condemned the behaviour of anthropologists with Native Americans. In his view anthropologists compile "useless knowledge for knowledge's sake" and do nothing to help Indian people, who have become objects for observation, "for experimentation, for manipulation, and for eventual extinction." "We are being researched to death!" anthropologists commonly hear in the Indian communities that close their doors to researchers (Kral and Idlout, 2006: 56). Lawrence Wylie, who produced the highly respected monograph *Village in the Vaucluse* in the late 1950s, upset the villagers who felt belittled and betrayed once they got hold of a copy of the book (Ouroussoff, 2001: 30). Nancy Scheper-Hughes (2001) similarly published a celebrated ethnography that sparked anger in the Irish village where she did her fieldwork in 1974. Returning to the village twenty years after the publication she attempted to apologise, only to get expelled. She had created, in her own words, an "unwanted" and "new species of traitor and friend, the anthropologist" (Robben and Sluka, 2007: 181). Indeed. "Do you mean to say that we're primitive people?," an officer asks Kim (2002: 81) in the United States. "Have you met enough primitives in Pinetown?" Stoller (1989: 90) met people in a Nigerian village of sorcerers who felt that Jean Rouch's films did not portray them in a favourable light; six years later one of them told him, "We don't like films. We don't want strangers laughing at us." Intrusions lead to pathetic situations that highlight the crying lack of basic reciprocity. Chagnon (1974: 111) was "chased around the village on a number of occasions by irate people wielding clubs and firebrands" because he was attempting to photograph cremations.

Spies

In today's postcolonial era however, tourist or spy costumes are not easy to wear. Anthropologists are increasingly denied access to developing countries. The "natives" are most of the time literate and have grown suspicious (rightly so) of what is written about them (Shuttleworth, 2004: 47; Harvey, 2004: 179; Robben and Sluka, 2007: 9, 19). As their publication pressures force them into pretence, spies develop "a type of schizophrenia" (Nuttall, 2007: 331). Berreman (1972: xxix) "[conceals] the extent of [his] note-taking, doing most of it at night or in private." A teacher asks Forsey (2004: 59) what it feels like to be a spy at a union meeting. Muir's (2004: 196) fieldwork "also felt like spying." Cauvin-Verner (2007: 201) was seen "as a sort of spy working for the Moroccan state [or] the United Nations (...) depending on the situation." Birckhead (2004: 98, 106) feels "like a voyeur, not much better than the reporters, television crews, and curiosity seekers whom [he] came to despise"; he has underestimated "how guilty and out of place [he] would sometimes feel." Lynne Hume feels that she is an "unnecessary presence" in her Yarrabah community—"yet another white researcher coming to probe into their lives, to ask questions, and then to leave" (Hume and Mulcock, 2004: xiii). Studying prostitution in Mexico, Kelly (2004: 6) wonders: "How dare I bother these people for my own selfish interests?" Elenore Smith Bowen's (1954: 290) moral dilemmas spring "from the very nature of [her] work, which had made [her] a trickster: one who seems to be what he is not and professes faith that he does not believe." Other researchers feel more at ease with their status. Chagnon (1974: 115) inserts an inexpensive earphone plug that automatically turns off the speaker of a recorder, and thanks to which he can "transcribe very juicy and very secret information while sitting in the middle of a crowd of people—provided that the earphone jack does not accidentally come out!" Recounting how the anthropology of Japan eroded and terminated her long-term friendship with Sachiko after involving her in research, Joy Hendry (1992: 170) is content with admitting that she "[brings] home better ethnography with which to impress [her] anthropological *nakama* ['inside group'], and [she] leaves Sachiko to continue her life." The lives and feelings of informants matter, but perhaps not as much as the anthropological careers they made possible.

"Hit and run" intrusions are probably seldom driven by philanthropic or humanitarian interests, and researchers often leave the field as they entered it—as strangers. When her fieldwork is over, Judith Okely (1992: 16–17) visits the Gipsy families she believes she has befriended, but is conned of her earrings. She has become "an ignorant and despised outsider again." And she accepts her responsibility in passing, with some vague reluctance, noting that "the anthropologist hardly respects the other's right to remain silent" (Okely, 1992: 22). Going further, expanding on the disrespect this remark underlies, would almost certainly mean renouncing anthropology. Put another way, failures of integration, and the guilt they produce, condition anthropology. Guilt is that by which anthropology struggles to exist. Kathleen Stewart (2007: 37) expresses this condition, perhaps unintentionally yet very forcefully—the embarrassment that uninvited anthropologists, like Yan Geling's (2006) banquet bugs, cause; the loneliness or exclusion that might only amuse themselves; and the implicit demonstration, as nothing much is happening, that there is *nothing to say*:

> The anthropologists keep doing the fun things they do together, poking around. They knock on the doors of the little fishermen's huts on the frozen lake. They invite themselves in for a visit and sit down on the bench inside. But the fishermen don't say a thing. Not even "Who are you?" or "What are you doing here?" So they sit together in a wild, awkward silence staring down through the hole in the ice to the deep, dark waters below.

When the very fact of describing "culture" contributes to its making, and when there is nothing to say that would not sound tautological, ethnography generates too many words and at the same time not enough of them. Too many, because culture does not need to be retold or rewritten to exist "out there"; not enough, because culture to even exist needs to be discursively shaped by us. So words are both pointless and scarce, empty signifiers and fragments of reality put together in an incessant search to complete it. Confronted with the very same kind of nothingness, Rethmann's (2007: 46) experience goes beyond awkwardness—distress, shame, and a general sensation of failure are conjured up. Can silence be explained? How, and why should one write it? How is she to "come up with interesting ethnographic details" in an empty Siberian space?

Fancy dresses

Most anthropologists have no choice but to promote their production of ethnographic knowledge, regardless of their degree of integration in the community. Some, like Pallí Monguilod (2001: 193–194), decide to compensate the unexciting realities of the field with fables of integration. Via her metaphors of cannibalism and vampirism, whereby she consumes gypsies and scientists and offers herself to be consumed, Pallí Monguilod refers to ideal-types of collaborative research and total immersion; but such *incorporation* remains wishful thinking! She may only "start desiring being one of them," "[long] for belonging," and beg them to "please bite [her] neck." The interpretive approach of Clifford Geertz (1973: 14, 357) cultivates such "cannibal-isle fantasizing"—a sort of "epistemological empathy" or "experimental mind reading." Pallí Monguilod's aspiration to stuff herself with culture, binge drink its spirit, or sniff its essence, corresponds to Marcus' (1992: xiv) project of transforming one's identity by incorporating the subjects' forms of speaking in one's own. Eating each other, why not ... but I am afraid the parallel is weak. Anthropologists are professional intruders whereas vampires (at least Bram Stoker's *Dracula*), will not enter a dwelling without being explicitly invited. Worse, according to MacCannell (1992: 66) cannibalism incorporates otherness

> in the most direct way, not merely by doing away with it, but by taking it in completely, metabolizing it, transforming it into shit, and eliminating it. The metabolized "other" supplies the energy for auto-eroticism, narcissism, economic conservatism, egoism, and absolute group unity or fascism, now all arranged under a positive sign.

Metaphoric or reflexive cannibalism produces a "utopian vision of profit without exploitation" that protects capitalism "from having to admit its own gruesome excesses" of domination (MacCannell, 1992: 20, 28). Such ingestion and digestion of the other might not be a very good idea then, not least because it is too fantastic to be of any use. But anthropologists still seek to be "swallowed" by the field, so instead of just relying on Pallí Monguilod's purely textual devices, they wear real disguises. They go for military camouflage or spotted fur, and like chameleons and stick insects, blend into the jungle. David-Néel (2008) dresses as a poor wanderer in Tibet, Norris (1993: 131) uses police jargon and dresses in the in-house style so that officers unaware of his research role take him for another officer, etc. Exoticism consists in becoming other and this less noble approach, "endoticism," in becoming *the* other (Michel, 2004: 145). The theatricality of anthropology comes into play as researchers, in their successful disguises, ape the Other (a temptation that travel guides, by and large, suggest we resist). They do not hesitate to lionise themselves as champions of integration who managed to emulate cultural features and overcome difficulties or sacrifice themselves. Their feeling of domination over the community they observe is often perceptible in unspoken claims that they are talented actors. Such "excesses" of integration are literally *in-credible*: integration should not be possible, yet it supposedly occurs, and as it does, generates guilt.

For example, George and Louise Spindler introduce one of Napoleon Chagnon's (1974: vii, ix) accounts of the Yąnomamö, in a foreword, as "the honest and very frank report of how one man became so much part of the Yąnomamö way of doing things that he could not extricate himself from this relationship except on Yąnomamö terms." Chagnon emerges as a hero who, through "deep personal involvement," survived excessive integration "to achieve the most meaningful goals in field research." Gerald Berreman (1972: xvii, xxxiii) "won villagers' confidence" following the initial struggles and disappointments, by being "uncritical, circumspect and meticulous about maintaining their trust." He "concealed such alien practices as [his] use of toilet paper" and "took up smoking as a step to increase rapport." He also simulated a liking for the local food and, "even more heroically, [he] concealed [his] distaste for the powerful home-distilled liquor." Powdermaker (1967: 110) managed to overcome her shame of dancing with the savages of her Melanesian "Stone-Age society":

> Something happened. I forgot myself and was one with the dancers. Under the full moon and for the brief time of the dance, I ceased to be an anthropologist from a modern society. I danced.

Dance, as Kazantzaki's Zorba tells his companion, overcomes language barriers. But this revelation betrays veiled condescension rather than an ecstatic experience. I wish the dance made her revise her conception of modernity, and step outside of her frame of Western "science"! In the same vein, Armstrong (1993: 19) enjoyed the company of hooligans so much that

> at times [he] felt guilty that [he] was not being more academic in approach. At time [he] laughed so much [he] almost cried; [he] was more than once the worse for drink.

Guilt in this example surfaces, like the tip of an iceberg, out of an excess of integration that seems to disqualify the researcher as a member of another (namely academic) species. To wash his guilt away, Armstrong (1993: 17–18) stresses that he has "cultural competence" to participate in this gathering. In his own words:

> I sought to be detached, but I was able to bring to the research a degree of reflexivity. The task of a researcher must always be to "fit in" and act as

naturally as possible. This I found no problem in doing. (...) It is, perhaps, "not done" in academia to say so, but when researching with groups of people, the primary aim is to be both known and popular.

This portrait of the anthropologist as a celebrity has soothing effects on researchers. Health advisers felt threatened by Parker's (2001: 146) presence at their clinic because she was "doing many aspects of their work as well as they themselves." Guilt conveniently evaporates towards inborn cultural sensitivity, acting talents, technical adaptability, and whatever one wishes to put under the "reflexivity" umbrella. Kathleen Stewart (1996: 69) explains how her strength of character and self-conscious performance as a field professional dodged gut feelings:

> Where the social worker's code expressed defensive disengagement from the hills, mine was expansive, engaged, appropriative. Where hers rested in visceral reaction, mine, armed with the spirit of adventure and a relativist chant, forcefully subverted visceral reaction in an act of transcendent self-reflection and the poetics of encounter.

When I read passages like this one, or like Chagnon's, Powdermaker's, and others, I can never evaluate how much is meant to entertain the reader, and how much expresses genuine self-importance. Are they aware that their adventures might be read, and in my opinion will mostly be read, at face value? How can I know, without asking Stewart here, and Cauvin-Verner earlier, and all the others? And if I ask, will I get a tongue-in-cheek answer? Writing inevitably entails a distortion of reality, especially because what authors choose to focus on and what they choose to omit is conditioned by the desire to tell a good story, as well as the demands of the publishing industry of the era in which they are writing. Hence researchers tend to include the exaggerations and small lies that will beautify their stories. They are professionals of the fib, forgers of the exotic—adventurers but also "inventurers" (Michel, 2004: 133–134).

Inventurers appear reflexive when they invoke specific skills such as the above (creative metaphorising, popularity, spirit of adventure, transcendent self-reflection...), and/or a vaguer "training" or "professionalism" (the kind of which is obviously unclear), and/or their awareness of influential anthropological literature. Reflexivity, to reiterate, usually stands for strategic guilt management. For example, Creighton (2007: 398) senses "a possible need to legitimize" her drinking with an Ainu informant and cites Malinowski, who wrote that it can be good, sometimes, to leave your notes and fully participate in what is going on. Seriously? Kim (2002: 157) states that he has "developed both a reflexive attitude and an ability to look at Koreans and their culture objectively." Should I take this literally? First, I believe it takes some effort to buy into these reflexive pantomimes. Non-anthropologists are likely to find such exaggerations, just like unimpressive or overstated fancy dresses, risible. And in fact overdressed researchers happen to be mocked. Okely (1996: 20–21) unlearns her accent, changes clothes and demeanour, and tells people that she works for charity. To preserve her relationship with the Gypsies she studies, she maintains this attitude in front of visiting friends who find it "both comical and unnecessary." When Anderson (2006: 50) joins in a banter using the word "motherfucker" like "some of the regulars," an informant reprimands him: "You didn't go to school for no eight years to talk like that!" Secondly, what happens when you are neither known nor popular? Worse, when you can hardly sympathise with the group you study?

It is only when relations are inverted, when researchers become researched, when reciprocity at last occurs, that anthropologists understand the violence of their practices. When Hastrup's (1992: 122) life and ethnographic work were staged in a Danish play, she would "never forget the pain resulting from having been fieldworked upon." In this respect, Crapanzano (2004: 5) underscores a moral and political responsibility to listen to others, "not only in terms of what they have to say about themselves but also what they have to say about us [anthropologists]." The ethics of integration constitute the ultimate challenge in anthropology, that which carves the face of research and determines its nature. I find it worrying and somewhat exciting that such ethics are negotiated in the context of mutual deception that I outline now.

No sincerity

Mutual deception

The naivety of first encounters between anthropologists and informants is nearly enshrined in situations of *mutual deception*. Michel Leiris (1988: 131) was not fooled by the nature of the relation between the "hypocritical European" and the "hypocritical Dogon" sharing drinks—"the only bond that exists between us is a joint falseness." "By instinct," Coquilhat writes, "[informants] feel the urge to deceive you." But to verify the reliability of information, Coquilhat (quoted in Fabian, 2000: 207) uses the same stratagem:

> Often I even affirm the contrary of what I was told by a preceding interlocutor. If the native is caught unawares, that is, if he thinks that I don't care, he will correct me with the exact answer and I will be satisfied for the time being. I will then repeat my inquiry with another individual.

The situation seems disrespectful and sad; yet it typifies the business of ethnographic methods, as common now as it was then. Paul Rabinow (1977: 29–30, 47) sees his Arabic teacher Ibrahim as a friend, while in Ibrahim's eyes Rabinow is but a resource. This most basic manifestation of otherness upsets the author who at the same time acknowledges (perhaps too obliquely or reluctantly) his involvement in deception, his contribution to the inequity of a relationship in which "the informant has only the foggiest notion of what this strange foreigner is really after." Rabinow's naivety is perfectly echoed in Marjorie Shostak's (2000: 29–30) initial hope that "close friendships might develop during the course of our work," which only after a long time was shattered with the realisation that "neither close friendship nor a really spontaneous, open approach to the interviews would be forthcoming." Given the only reason of Crick's (1992: 179–183) presence in Sri Lanka was to get material for his book, he attempted to befriend Ali to assuage his own "exploitative role playing." But his guilt over using people also produced an impression that people were using him. Crick (1989: 34–35, 1992: 174) understands the fragile and forced exchanges between researcher and informant as what Hatfield has called "mutual exploitation." Scheper-Hughes (2000) has a very similar take on participant observation: "We are at the mercy of those who agree to take us in as much as they are at our mercy in the ways we represent them." Role playing, exemplified by Briggs (1970) and Shostak (2000: 36) as they become the "daughter" of Eskimo "parents" and the "niece" of a !Kung "aunt," respectively, may also lead to romanticised accounts of the field (as part of a defence mechanism of guilt management that I have summarised above).

No honesty with informants

Anthropological relationships perhaps exclusively fall within acts of self-presentation theorised by Erving Goffman (1959), and hypocrisy. "One can really only pretend to be a friend," contends Joy Hendry (1992: 170). Kelly

(2004: 7) lies to neighbours, acquaintances, and her informants' relatives, creating stressful situations of inauthenticity and alienation. Even when anthropologists believe they have secured true friendships, they might feel "prevented by loyalty," as in Lee's (2006: 33) case, "from discussing topics such as social interactions in the depth that [they] otherwise might." Lee experiences "pangs of conscience" because she cannot say the whole truth. Her friendship, "like any other, requires self-censorship." Muir (2004: 196) admits that "few people understood how much of what they did and said outside of interview and workshop settings could be included in [his] study." Recording human activity arouses guilt, however deep the connection with informants. As Gearing (1995: 206) uses information provided by her partner for example, she feels as though she is "cheating," taking a short cut rather than showing ethnographic expertise. Briggs (1970: 20) tells an important female informant that she wants to be adopted to live like an Eskimo. "Embarrassed by the scholarly analytical aspect of the [anthropological] enterprise, thinking she would consider it prying," Briggs decides to conceal from her that she will be studying them. In a footnote, John Van Maanen (1988: 97) avows his misbehaviour before concluding that "hypocrisy is always at issue in fieldwork":

> I was once thanked by some of my police acquaintances for coming to the funeral of one of their mates. I still feel like a hypocrite recalling the incident, since I was at the funeral to unravel a cultural rite and not to pay my respects.

To stay in this very fitting religious vein, Birckhead's (2004: 99) mood was affected by "the guilt and 'bad faith' (Sartre, 1953: 47) of being 'Brother Jimmy,' who sought to absorb their spiritual meanings and convert these into social science schemas." Hortense Powdermaker (1967: 9) has famously stressed that the fieldworker must move back and forth between involvement and detachment. But such "participant observation" is an oxymoron (Rabinow, 1977: 79; Stoller, 1989: 155; Robinson, 2004: 163) or a tautology for the anthropologist's "lack of method" (Crapanzano, 1972: 17), which arouses many dilemmas and much guilt. Here Van Maanen and Birckhead's hypocritical sentiments come with the realisation that the "professional stranger" (Agar, 1980), who is supposed to "step in and out" of other cultures and make this impossible operation possible, cannot maintain her distance and fresh glance in the long run. Integration is bound to become more excessive and more unethical over time.

There is a whiff of self-flagellation in these notes. Anthropologists know that what they do is "wrong," but they do it anyway. They resign themselves to their methodological suicide. The complacent methodological texts that recommend, for instance, that ethnographers be "candid about their tasks, explaining what they plan to study and how they plan to study it" (Fetterman, 1989: 130) merely undermine the plausibility of the inductive approach. As commendable the virtues of sincerity or integrity may sound, they are not so realistic in the field. We all have hidden agendas ranging from status recognition to strategies for seducing the beloved, and we do not always make our intentions public. Instead, we proudly show our hypocritical smile and deceive each other in some way or another (Hammersley and Atkinson, 1995: 264). In his study of part-time crime, Jason Ditton (1977: 10) is candid about the unethicality of participant observation "by virtue of being interactionally deceitful. It does not become ethical merely because this deceit is openly practiced. It only becomes inefficient." The traditional and impossible recommendation that the anthropologist be simultaneously inside and outside was meant to be transgressed. The traps that Jeanne Favret-Saada (1980: 18) has learnt to avoid like plague, namely "that of agreeing to 'participate' in the native discourse, and that of succumbing to the temptations of subjectivism," eventually enable most of her findings.

No honesty with anthropologists

Unlike Leiris who became quite critical of colonialism, Marcel Griaule suggested that the ethnographer proceed with the assumption that natives are lying (Hand, 2004: 59). Nisa told Marjorie Shostak (2000: 28), during their last meeting, "something [she] found so puzzling that [she] began to doubt not only it but much of what [Nisa] had told [her] before." Margaret Kenna (1992: 150) on her Greek island "was naïve enough not to realise that people would, and did, deliberately lie to [her]." In the conversations Crapanzano (1980: 14, 150) had with Tuhami, "it was often impossible to distinguish what was real from what was dream and fantasy, hallucination and vision." There was also "something seductive in his discourse." Such "ethnographic seduction," as Robben (1996) calls it, forces fieldworkers to ponder some rather intricate issues of manipulation. Talking to military officers and victims of political persecution in Argentina, Robben received pressures from both parties and had the task of "resisting the seductive manoeuvres that tried to draw [him] emotionally into one camp." For him, an ethnographer always runs the risk of adhering to a surface discourse which, "disguised in a seductive cloak," aims to induce guilt—for example, "I have told you my story so that you can write the truth." In his *Manual of Ethnography*, Marcel Mauss (1926: xxx) lists the dangers of "superficial observation" as follows: "do not 'believe'. Do not believe that you know because you have seen it. Do not pronounce moral judgement. Do not be amazed. Do not fly into a rage." These words of caution refer to the many cases in which manipulation infuriates researchers. Paul Stoller (1989: 127) among the Songhay of Niger discovered "to his disgust" that "everyone had lied to [him], and that the data [he] had so laboriously collected were worthless." When Chagnon (1974: 16) learnt that his guides came along "for a machete, an axe, and a large cooking pot," and had no intention of reaching the destination (and do not actually go any further), he was "so furious that [he] refused to let any of them have any of the game that [he] shot." His laborious interviews confuse him as well as his informants, eventually making everyone angry. The quality of his data improves on later field trips, as he arranges interviews "so that no single informant [spends] more than three or so hours at one sitting" (Chagnon, 1974: 57–62). He does not seem to wonder what a three-hour questioning must feel like! Upon his arrival in Nuer territory early in 1930, Evans-Pritchard (1940: 9–12) is already persuaded that "their country and character are alike intractable," and that he will "fail to establish friendly relations with them." And indeed the Nuer are at first "unusually hostile, for their recent defeat by Government forces and the measures taken to ensure their final submission [have] occasioned deep resentment." Evans-Pritchard is the enemy, this representative of Western power that they will refuse to assist. They ignore him, show disgust at his presence, and only visit him in rare occurrences to ask for tobacco. Finding himself "almost entirely cut off from communication with [them]," the anthropologist is incapable of establishing trust. His inquiries are constantly sabotaged. He gives an example of a conversation with an individual who simply wants to know (apparently) how his information will be used. But this is sufficient for Evans-Pritchard (1940: 13) to conclude: "I defy the most patient ethnologist to make headway against this kind of opposition. One is just driven crazy by it"; and for this conclusion to inspire the "Nuerosis" pun (see further).

I find Evans-Pritchard and Chagnon's examples truly fascinating, insofar as their lack of empathy would be regarded, today, as *literally* crazy. In other words, you and I understand that they are *out of their mind* as soon as they see pathology, irrationality, and unruly behaviour in what would qualify for us as normality, rationality, and control. Yet clearly, more recent anthropology reproduces, despite its goodwill of escaping colonial relations, the same "naïve" approaches (since they do not disappear with time, I feel authorised to judge them so). Cauvin-Verner (2007: 201) "asked many questions without official endorsement," and "no one in Zagora recognised [her] status of ethnologist." These are not great conditions to start with, and yet she was at first surprised that people "evaded [her] questions, or made things up, or refused to talk about certain topics." She did not seem to consider what they would gain from her curiosity and tenacity, nor imagine how she would feel if they subjected her to the same constant questioning. Her own conclusion was not yet commonplace in pre-colonial times perhaps, but in view of African history seems a little pathetic: "I did not know yet that the right to interview must be acquired, and that the tone of the questionnaire inhibits communication." Her fieldwork in the desert shows how tourists and guides deceive each other (as well as themselves) in pursuit of their own agendas. And it does so even better if the anthropologist's own practices, ironically, already perform what they seek to understand! To analyse what I do, I can either carry a mirror with me wherever I go; or better, ask people to study me (through lengthy questionnaires of course, just to ensure they are bearable).

No respect

Compassion

Facing the indeterminacy of its role and object, in pursuit of moving horizons, anthropology finds many reasons to feel guilty. The jargon of the field seems disrespectful, whether it addresses "informants" or even "others." "Informant," a key term of colonialism, reduces knowledge to an amount of information given and received (Hours and Selim, 2010: 214), and people to information providers. And what does "other" mean, if not a faceless embodiment of difference, an anonymity deprived of history and identity, unlike the ethnographer who writes herself through this other? Besides, according to MacCannell (1992: 66),

> [t]he use of the term "other" (small "o") promotes the self, ego, the first person singular, by pretending to do the opposite; that is, by bringing up "the other." The unmarked, undifferentiated "other" is nothing other than the self-interested expression of ego masked with sociability.

Embarrassed about the inappropriateness of their lexicon, anthropologists use alternatives—locals, natives, indigenes, respondents, and the like. Fears of ethnocentrism and parochialism exacerbate such political correctness and prevent researchers from recognising similarities between themselves and the people they study. Focusing on alterity may have "*the consequence of denying to others the complexity which we impute to ourselves*" (Cohen, 1992: 223) and "disguise an implicit assumption of the subordinate status of those studied" (Gearing, 1995: 210). When people's complexities and aspirations are ignored, they become foils to researchers, objects instead of subjects, conceptual bricks instead of concept makers. Already suffering from violence, cruelty, poverty, madness, and despair, people become in addition "the objects of self-interested professional and disciplinary quarrels and abstractions" (Biehl, Good, and Kleinman, 2007: 13). Michel (2004: 72, 77) cites Henri Michaux (1967: 25, 121), who in *A Barbarian in Asia* contends that "the white man possesses a quality that has enabled him to make his way: *disrespect*," even if "he has been seen, much more seen than he has seen." Shame on you, anthropologists? Are you not a bit quick to talk loftily about "*your* field," to claim your expertise on a land that is not yours, to mark your territory, your hunting ground, your playground?

Several avenues attempt to resist this tendency and take the form of autoethnographies, indigenous ethnographies, and life-history approaches such as *testimonios* (Reed-Danahay, 1997; Ellis, 2003, 2008; Hanson, 2004; Meneley and Young, 2005; Robben and Sluka, 2007: 17, 20; Chang, 2008; Muncey, 2010). A focus on the individual attempts to eschew the reifying effects of generalisation (Rapport, 2003)—narratives of people feeling pain, making choices, contradicting themselves, and so forth—is used "against culture," that is against their incarceration in a homogeneous time and space (Rapport, 2000: 89). Thus Crapanzano (1980) portrays Tuhami, Shostak (2000) focuses on Nisa, Harry Wolcott (2002) describes his relationship with a "sneaky kid" who based camp near his home, etc. Demonstrating respect for these lives, which are never set in stone but in constant flux, could shed light on their complexity. In this line of thought, a sort of "compassionate turn" has reasserted the importance of empathy and drawn anthropologists to studies of violence, human rights (Geertz, 2012: 187), sufferance (Robben and Sluka, 2007: 23–24), and social exclusion and repression (Jackson, 2005: 30).

The compassionate turn does not come as a surprise, the former "savages" of anthropology having today emerged as the most exploited, repressed, and traumatised people on earth (Bourgois, 1991: 111). Biehl and Locke (2010) translate respect into listening, not as clinicians but as readers and writers, to these people; and analysing how clinical and political discourses interweave with "the sheer materiality of life's necessities." They advocate an "anthropology of becoming" that would distance itself from the traditional reliance on the explanatory power of the past, and concentrate instead on people's possible futures. Stoller (1989: 156) suggests along this line that respect is "born of deep immersion in other worlds [and] demands that nameless informants be portrayed as recognizable individuals who suffer defeats and win victories in their social worlds." Harvey (2004: 175, 180–181) promotes "guesthood," which wraps up reciprocal forms of "conversation, and even, perhaps, collaboration" and puts the anthropologist "into relational encounters requiring ethical behaviours that are simultaneously vital and vitalizing for academia and for our hosts." Jackson (2005: 31) more specifically favours a comparative "inter-experience" that places viewpoints on a similar footing: the anthropologist must find something in her own experience that approximates the experience of the other.

Exoticism

At the other extreme of the fear of ethnocentricism is another, that of exoticism. Blackwood (1995: 72) believes that ethnographic work is about "recognizing the bonds among us rather than reifying the difference to make Others exotic or inferior." She therefore seeks to "avoid the stance that exoticizes other cultures." But her own stance could lead to demagogy and idealism, for we are not "all the same" and it is all too simple to stigmatise exoticism while it represents (just like xenophobia) normal human reactions to the discovery of others. In fact, exoticism and ethnocentrism do not represent opposite extremes in the spectrum of human relations. Morton (1995: 170–171) even believes that they blend into shameful combinations. Attracted to Tongan men, she identifies in exoticism a racist current that frightens anthropologists. Attractions to physically and culturally different people, to the easily accessible and impressionable Other, echo the colonial exploitations anthropologists would rather forget about—as well as the sordid depravity of sexual tourism. The sexual relationships that Cauvin-Verner

(2007: 260–261) analyses, between female tourists and their Moroccan guides, are embedded with the most extreme and hateful forms of racism. Gearing (1995: 202–203) holds a different view. The exotic has always had "erotic appeal" and "feeling sexually attracted to the people we live among and study is a much more positive reaction than feeling repulsed by them." In my opinion, overall, the above accounts miss the point. To encounter Difference, if you are human, is to feel attractions (exoticism) and repulsions (racism) in often tangled ways. It is tempting to state that such feelings should not exist; but we all know they do! Perhaps they are not always as bad as they seem; but they can be! What does *not* exist, on the other hand, is the neutral acknowledgement of Difference, or its cool-headed celebration. And yet some well-rehearsed arguments on racism and exoticism still rely on this politically correct, moralizing myth, conveniently escaping from less comfortable realities. I would like the anthropologist to be braver. The do-gooder, self-righteous researcher ought to take risks, get out of her cowardly retreat and engage with taboos. I would like her to resist her own attractions, not to people, but to the safe and often sterile arguments that preserve her. Pointing out that racism and exoticism must be avoided does not help, because they cannot be. And deleting them from the dictionary does not make them disappear from the world. So rather than indulging in superficial oppositions ("attraction is positive, repulsion is negative") and facile prescriptions ("I must not exoticize the Other") or reflexivity ("I have exoticized the Other, shame on me"), this researcher must try and fathom *what her attractions (and/or repulsions) are made of.* She must face her fears, come to grips with their complex manifestations, and do her best to understand them. Erotic tension has made encounters between European explorers and "primitives" confusing and at times upsetting. But following Fabian (2000: 79), it simply characterises knowledge production as an ecstatic process. Repulsion and attraction are emotionally indivisible in the true erotic experience—an experience that Kulick and Willson's (1995) edited volume, by and large disregarding the history of sexuality, the philosophy of love, and psychoanalysis, fails to describe. Even liking or disliking people, as Robben's (1996) comment on ethnographic seduction shows, involves mixed feelings that make categorisations (e.g., the exotic, the racist, the attractive) unreliable in real life.

In consequence, I cannot but perceive idealism in situations of "respect" allegedly reached after ethnocentrism and exoticism were successfully defeated. By idealism I mean a somewhat sterile insistence on what ethnographic methods "should" achieve, not on the possibilities and intricacies of such achievements. On a more optimistic stance, idealism mirrors the potential of a discipline in perpetual search for itself. The next section indicates how pathological anthropology can become when people disappear from it, when integration is idealised rather than theorised *from*, and *for* these people.

Idealism

Impossible ethnographies

The main argument in this book was motivated by a plain but very disturbing observation. If one accepts that the most important aspect of anthropology is the quality of *communication* in general (and field relations in particular), then the happy encounter where both parties love each other must be more idealistic than realistic. Communication was "painstaking and partial" in Rabinow's (1977: 154–155) fieldwork, and its ruptures proved to be, despite the frustrations they brought about, "turning points." There are various and well-known ways in which the postmodern contribution and its developments rely on idealist assumptions. While postmodernism "questions the anthropologist's very 'right to write,'" it is for Geertz (2012: 195) "more a mood and an attitude than a connected theory." It has also proved to Rabinow (2008: 52) "more reactive than creative of new modes of inquiry or forms of writing." If only informants could speak without the intermediation of a fieldworker, if only this fieldworker could disappear, Rabinow (2008: 53) explains, then anthropology would finally realise its "dream of transparency"—its only point would be the "other."

A good interpretation does not know its author, because it is collaboratively built. In psychoanalysis the patient is the only true collaborator, according to Bion, since only she knows what it means to be herself, what it feels like to have ideas like hers (Ciccone and Ferrant, 2009: 113). In other words, communication between researchers and their subjects will not describe what subjects really feel. In a way then, anthropological methods are inevitably idealist. Take anthropology at home: to what extent can researchers merge the personal and the professional (Dyck, 2000: 49–50; Pink, 2000: 96), bear the costs entailed in transforming friends and relatives into informants, and vice versa? Take collaborative research, which claims that plural authorship fashions more authentic accounts: but the ethnographer does select, truncate, rearrange, edit stories towards her own thesis, her own story. The resulting text remains an asymmetrical *representation* (Clifford, 1988: 43–44). Dialogical anthropology and *poesis* reconfirm that writers represent natives out of their own interest (Tyler, 1992: 5). Furthermore participants, no matter how fascinating their lives appear, are very often unable or unwilling to write. Most will have no interest in ethnographic research (Horner, 2004: 17–18, 24). Does this mean that nothing should be reported about them, lest ethnography seem overly interpretive? Take Stoller's (1989: 56) "sensualised ethnographies" in which "the scenes described (people, interviews, ritual) become authors, the anthropologist becoming the intermediary between the author and an audience": how can events write themselves? Again, should the subject's refusal to speak not result in an absence of ethnographic interpretation (Josephides, 1997: 27)? Take multi-sited ethnography: George Marcus (1998) is not clear about how investigations in various and possibly incomparable locales ought to take place in practice (Muir, 2004: 186–187). Conversely, how useful is ethnography in just one site when the activities it describes are influenced by distant processes and agents? Because the field is as much characterised by *absences* as by presences, Amit (2000: 12) senses that it must be complemented with census data, archival documents, and more. To make the point that observations are likely to find their guiding principle *elsewhere*, to be the effects of a greater structure invisible *in situ*, Pierre Bourdieu (1993: 159) refers to American ghettos that define themselves in relation to an absence (essentially absence of the State, and of everything that goes with it: the police, schools, health institutions, associations, etc.). Fieldwork, in this respect, might always be less insightful than an examination of the distant powers that make sense of it. Some anthropologists find traditional fieldwork so problematic that they recommend historical approaches instead (Robben and Sluka, 2007: 17).

And finally take the notions of respect and reciprocity: participatory anthropology, Kral and Idlout (2006: 69) argue, is an indigenised form of research that "rests on the foundation of inclusiveness and respect"; but they do not delve into how this foundation is built. Seymour-Smith also remains vague when urging anthropologists "to perform some useful or valued service in return for the collaboration he or she requires" (Robben and Sluka, 2007: 9). Stoller (1989: 84) understands the decolonisation of anthropology as a "discourse in which the others classify their anthropologists in the same way that we classify them." But of course he only asks us to "imagine" such a discourse, precisely because these others are non-anthropologists who will never produce it. For Jackson (2005: 32), researchers must "go some way toward *overcoming our estrangement from others, finding some common ground, and working out ways in which coexistence is possible in a divided world.*" These researchers will achieve "a mere rhetoric of humanism" unless they are in practice, through direct and sometimes trying encounters, open to otherness. And yet, what sort of knowledge will very little "common ground" deliver? What happens when openness does not help, when fruitful interactions are not possible? And in this latter case, why overcome estrangement? In delineating the requirements of good communication, Jackson seems to point at the extent of anthropology's failure so far.

Manuals of ethnographic methods tend to tone down such failure, usually outlining ideal research conditions and vaguely referring to difficulties or impossibilities as inconveniences—which by definition one should quickly "apologise for" or "feel sorry about" and move on. For example, Van Maanen (1988: 80) suggests that an ethnographic study will be more trusted if fieldworkers show that they liked those they studied (and vice versa), even if there were certain periods that were dull and even distasteful. But these good fieldwork conditions draw on selected reports of ethnographic bliss, such as fieldwork among the Ndembu of Zambia, which in the words of Victor Turner's wife (1985: 4) "became our delight":

> Arriving at a distant village we would be greeted by the whole population, shaking hands and thumbs with us and clapping. I would find the women's kitchens, while Vic sat in the meeting hut with the men. (...) They liked Vic.

This slightly romanticised arrival invites the reader to experience it herself, to become an anthropologist. Yet innumerable accounts make it clear that the field is seldom philanthropic. In a footnote on his one-month stay among the Amphlett natives for instance, Malinowski (1922: 36) writes that he "found [them] surprisingly intractable and difficult to work with ethnographically." He later refers to them as "bad informants" (Malinowski, 1922: 293). I have included in this book other illustrations of frustrations and disappointments. How can we establish relationships with people we do not like (Robben and Sluka, 2007: 124)? What are the textual implications of such feelings towards them? How do we deal with the fact that different levels of integration will produce different truths? Why, in methodological texts (Van Maanen, 1988; Fetterman, 1989; Denzin, 1997; Brewer, 2000: 6) and elsewhere, this never-ending emphasis on sanitised settings in which people happily collaborate, to the detriment of more realistic circumstances?

Ideological populism

Horner (2004: 19–20) describes the tenacity of idealism in ethnographic methodology quite forcefully. He points to "the perpetual praise researchers give to the generosity of their informants" and "the qualms they express about the ethical status of their decisions" like so many indications that research is understood "in terms of idealist ethics rather than in terms of material conditions." It seems important to further explain why this is the case. The idealist bias, in my view, is a direct consequence of the management of guilt described above, as well as what Olivier de Sardan (2005) calls "ideological populism." Olivier de Sardan transferred the notion of populism, developed in a sociological study of domination (Grignon and Passeron, 1989), to the anthropology of development. Typified by the practices and rhetoric of non-governmental organisations, ideological populism refers to a relationship in which intellectuals enthusiastically discover the people, pity them or marvel at their potential, and eventually strive for enhancing their welfare. This kind of populism (which Olivier de Sardan distinguishes from the *methodological* populism he would recommend) exalts the cognitive, moral, and cultural virtues of people in accordance with the romantic ideas researchers have about these people and their resources. Further, anthropologists often oscillate between this optimistic ideology and its "miserabilist" opposite, which, focusing on processes of domination and exploitation, victimises people. While populism and miserabilism respectively overestimate and underestimate the autonomy of people, they arise from the same indignations drawing on the same stereotypes. The adulation of the merits of the people is easily converted into a denunciation of the deprivations they suffer. Both populism and miserabilism shape the demagogic attitude of a researcher who praises the culture under scrutiny to get rid of her responsibilities as intellectual—notably that of making a change and having a significant impact on people's lives. Confining herself to reassertions of the importance of "respect" and "tolerance," ideas that are always well-received but constantly violated, this paternalist researcher turns rural customs into model values, above the corruption of urban life; the uneducated person becomes authentic, and the "cultured" individual false (Maget, 1968: 1273).

Hours and Selim (2010: 14, 101–102) concur that a "developmentalist neo-colonialism" manages alterity just as 19th-century evolutionism used to. Philanthropic practices and discourses results from a desire, not to redistribute wealth, but to conspicuously display one's altruism, or a fine mix of goodwill and pity. Contemporary care is a charitable paternalism posing as the bulwark against the individualism of consumer society. While failing to create social links, it masks the unbridled competition of the market economy in charity galas—parodies of solidarity where wealth is supposed to turn into generosity. Distress, Luc Boltanski (2007: 189) notices in the same vein, has become "an opportunity for entertainment. Through the upsurge of charity, mass hedonist culture reasserts itself." So let us recognise the Western tradition of a deliberate search for the spectacle of sufferance, not to relieve it, but:

> to live the precious moment of emotion and (...) joy it arouses: "we would gladly make people miserable so we can taste the sweetness of pitying them" writes Mrs Riccoboni to Garrick in 1769, from Paris, in a letter that portrays the Parisian trend of sensitivity.

Baudelaire ironically commented after Sade on the hypocrisy of noble feelings; Nietzsche saw pity as a disease; and I think the philosophy of Sade helped me sublimate my own guilt, in the field and in life, towards more humane and passionate relations with the people I meet. To make sense of my research activities, I first needed to accept the monster within me.

3
Water

Abstract: *Taking its cue from the conclusions of Chapter 2, this chapter reverts to the autobiographical style of Chapter 1. After arguing for an anthropology of sensual experience, which must strive to transcribe passions, it links Jean-Paul Sartre's* Nausea *to my own experience of fieldwork in an advertising agency.*

Along with this experience, characterised by miscommunication and abjection (or the intrusive integrations of Chapter 2), other fields shape comparably passionate feelings—hatred in Burkina Faso and the United Kingdom; love in South Korea.

Eroticism emerges from abjection, which may develop from a lack of cultural knowledge, but it is also the true form of communication and inspiration of emotional anthropology—whether in France, in Greece, or somewhere in the sky above Asia, light as a feather.

Bouchetoux, François. *Writing Anthropology: A Call for Uninhibited Methods.* New York: Palgrave Macmillan, 2014. DOI: 10.1057/9781137404176.0006.

Ethnogastritis: back to the future

On my field

Murakami's (2006) "Nausea 1979" sketches the idea that we accumulate knowledge that we are not aware of, since it might be revealed by accident, sometimes a long time after acquisition. I have cited this passage above:

> So, what you're telling me, Mr Murakami, is that my own guilt feelings—feelings of which I myself was unaware—could have taken on the form of nausea or made me hear things that were not there?

The person who slept with his friends' partners "forgot" the guilt feelings that occupied his mind (however temporarily); and in the vomit these feelings metaphorically reappeared. He rejected the "evils" he already knew about but had been thus far "hidden from view," so to speak. The nausea is to him what the dream is to Freud (1991: 69)—something that he knew and remembered, but that was "beyond the reach of [his] waking memory." An abject manifestation of the unconscious in this case, indigestion embodies a moral transgression. Fieldwork in my experience has more to do with, and more to gain from, such transgressive feelings and practices. Integration emerges from an initial "intrusion," the forbidden incisions and dissections of modern medicine. The fever of guilt that accompanies intrusion is not purely debilitating however; it can be positively (rather than apologetically) channelled towards better anthropology. To make this point and concentrate on the subjectivity of the researcher, the paper must return to the "I," notwithstanding the headaches and nausea "I" will bring about.

If you ask me what ethnography is for, I will feel embarrassed. And instead of elaborating as condensed or straightforward an answer as possible, I would rather report what constitutes such embarrassment. In 2005 I spent three months working in the creative department of a French advertising agency. Whereas I got along with marketing people, I felt much less comfortable with the creatives. We "respected" each other but did not like each other. This respect did not make much sense in my understanding of ethnography—I perceived it as a circumlocution of "truth" that discredited my analysis with the force of a determinism. At the same time, a positive attitude towards informants would as much bias my field notes as a negative one. Had I loved my creatives, I would have embellished their portraits and my research would not have been more trustworthy.

Sensuality

The far-from-ideal degree of socialisation I reached in the organisation made me think harder about the relations I entertained with myself (subjectivity), with others (sociability), and more pertinently with *myself amongst others*—it made me think about the conditions of communication and integration in the field, and about the role and possibilities of authorship in writing. My experience of fieldwork had nothing to do with the pleasures of dressing-up mentioned earlier. On the contrary it was permeated with self-disgust. I would rather speak for others, but was restricted to a sickening egocentrism. I could never get out of myself. I had to manage, therefore, this guilt I have described so far, hoping to find a cure to my overdose of self. In the light of the "puppeteering" critique above, I think it is worth describing this process more fully, lingering on one illustration rather than connecting theoretical snippets.

In recent anthropology "the body as a site of knowledge has been rediscovered" (Fabian, 2000: 8). In his monumental but complex work, Maurice Merleau-Ponty (1945: 216, 239) explains that "it is through my body that I understand the other, just as it is through my body that I perceive 'things.'" In experiencing the world as it appears to me, I reclaim my body, I rediscover my "self," that is the natural subject of my perception. In his "Senses" chapter, Michael Herzfeld (2001: 240–253) argues that the Cartesian separation of mind and body led to an overreliance on the visual and the verbal that dismisses smell, touch, and taste. He calls for an anthropology of sensual experience inspired by Marshall McLuhan and Walter J. Ong. Paul Stoller (1989: 24–25, 135–136, 153, 155) draws on Jacques Derrida's reading of "On experience," one of Montaigne's *Essays* (book III), to contend that ethnography should not separate the intelligible from the sensible. Ethnography must be empirical, literary, evocative. While scientific methods and theories are usually more highly valued than vivid description, phenomenology shows that they obscure rather than enlighten our perception and understanding of life. In this way "lifeless texts constitute (...) the large majority of anthropological works." Instead, one should attempt to write passions. For example, the disgusting should be "spit out into an ethnographic text" with sensual intensity, just like the concept of vomit engages in Derrida's writings the "chemical" senses of taste and smell. By the same token, Harry Wolcott (2005) depicts fieldwork as an artistic method and Michael Jackson (2005: 178) as an empirical "art of dialogue," which subverts abstract concepts to immerse itself in the worlds of others and create the conditions of tolerant communication. With reference to Maurice Merleau-Ponty and others, Michael Jackson's (1996, 2005) volumes explore phenomenological directions for anthropology. While our relations with others form the core of human existence, this existence, this lived reality "*is grasped only within ourselves*" and cannot be inferred from its discursive constructions (Jackson, 2005: xxviii, 140).

Human viruses

The hostile African climate and unusual diseases contributed to drive explorers "out of their minds," as Fabian (2000) puts it. During Jérôme Becker's first night on the African continent in the 1880s, "one attack of nausea follows the other" and the crisis eased towards dawn "only to make room for fever, that terrible African fever" (Fabian, 2000: 62). The unresponsive Nuer gave Evans-Pritchard (1940: 13) such a hard time that he humorously suggested that one displays symptoms of "Nuerosis" after spending a few weeks with them. Alfred Métraux (quoted in Rivière, 2010: 164) acutely summarises the whole crisis of anthropology in a letter to Pierre Verger, with the idea that people (including ourselves) make us sick:

> Through an act of masochism and pure stupidity, I have spent a month wandering around the Aymara country (...) the Aymara Indians inspire physically in me a violent aversion. In fact, they give me nausea.

As such, nausea is both ordinary in the field and intensified by extraordinary relationships with strangers. The psychosomatic aspects of fieldwork are crucial to our understanding of anthropology. Take one of Paul Rabinow's (1977: 45) episodes in Morocco: Ali insists that Rabinow attend a wedding despite his suffering from a stomach virus. After an argument in the car on the way back, Ali gets off. Leaving Ali to walk the remaining five miles to Sefrou, Rabinow was "confused, nauseous, and totally frustrated." Ethnographic writing never comes out intact from such field relations. Muir (2004: 185) includes "ethnographic dis-ease" in his title, evocative of Stephen Tyler's (1992: 5) aphorism: "Writing is an illness we cannot treat but only recover from." For Geertz (1988: 71), the experimental movement in ethnographic writing even amounts to "epistemological hypochondria." What sort of writing does nausea produce?

Nausea 1938

The diary form was not seen, before the consecration of realist ethnography as "science," as unscientific. It was quite the opposite. Many authors felt that a travelogue would be more spontaneous and more objective than the rearranged, crafted, descriptive, and in the end fictionalised presentation of less personal monographs. Coquilhat, Capelo, and Ivens were among those who reasoned that "the diary was a more realistic mode of representation than edited narratives and descriptions" (Fabian, 2000: 248–249). Such understanding is also, in my opinion, what makes Leiris' (1934) account so astonishing. The diary form, Michael Taussig (2003) tells us, "seems more real than the flimsy thing we call experience." If Taussig lost his diary, he would lose himself, because the diary says, "*I have been here. I exist. This happened. A mark in time.*" And of course the diary directly comes to grips with some challenges of subjectivity I have already outlined. These challenges have been raised by Jean-Paul Sartre's (1981) early work *Nausea*.

Sartre believed that only the diary form could express something between the concept and the feeling—what he called a "real-life experience." *Nausea* is the diary of Antoine Roquentin (Sartre's voice), for whom a real-life experience should be fixed *at once*, effortlessly:

> I do not need to make phrases. I write to bring certain circumstances to light. Beware of literature. I must follow the pen, without looking for words. (Sartre, 1981: 68)

One must write without looking for words and jot down whatever comes to mind, along the lines of André Breton's (1933) "automatic" writing that disregards coherence, grammar, even vocabulary. Of Freudian inspiration, this technique aims to release the forgotten memories and abilities dwelling in the unconscious. The transposition of a real-life experience into Roquentin's journal, however, is tantalising because inscription generates a strangeness that recedes from experience:

> The best thing would be to write down events from day to day. Keep a diary to see clearly—let none of the nuances or small happenings escape even though they might seem to mean nothing. And above all, classify them. (...) For instance, here is a cardboard box holding my bottle of ink. (...) Well, it's a parallelepiped rectangle, it opens—that's stupid, there's nothing I can say about it. This is what I have to avoid, I must not put in strangeness where there is none. I think that is the big danger in keeping a diary: you exaggerate everything. You continually force the truth because you're always looking for something. (Sartre, 1981: 5)

Roquentin may accept the logic of automatic writing but at the same time remains suspicious of literature. He points out that thinking about what to write already distorts experience. There is *nothing to say* about this inkpot. As I worked on my monograph I identified this risk of "lying to yourself" that Roquentin underlines here; an ever-present risk of coming up with words that do not even speak the author's mind. Recording sensations entails thinking about how to best express them, but thinking "too much" unduly twists the familiar into the unfamiliar, and upsets memory. Thus I tend to describe things not the way I perceived them, but the way I would like to remember them. What I am feeling now, for instance, is that my lack of confidence affects my writing as I write. I can remember people's actions and reactions in a recent past, but it all seems too ephemeral, too spontaneous for me to fix it into writing. And if I persist in my struggle to capture memories, I feel like contaminating them, even more so when they are diluted into "theory" or academic requirements. Then I reassure myself, thinking that reconstruction is not necessarily a perversion; just the *sine qua non* of writing.

Roquentin is suspicious of himself, of the "I," and I, like him, identify the enemy of my ethnography study—myself. I have confessed, incautiously perhaps, my self-hatred as I wrote the field. Let me try to remember how exactly it happened. Many people in the advertising agency, including myself, made me sick. Everything we did seemed absurd. What was I doing here? I talked rubbish with these people, listened to their conversations, and watched their predictable actions. I heard their keyboards rattling, and saw the disgusting prose their printers belched out and the ugly images left over in the dustbin. Looking up I could see finished posters proudly displayed on the wall. All this hustle and bustle for *this*... When it was time to organise field notes towards some kind of narrative coherence, I had to "analyse" *this*. Analysis—what a bizarre word. How is analysis different from field notes? Can it be anything else than the diary of my diary? I felt unnecessary. There was too much of myself yet I must face myself. And I disliked writing, but it was part of my job and I could only hope that readers would find the execrable exhibitionism of my moods and doubts and little complaints tolerable.

To what extent, in such conditions, is it possible to *think* the other? What do "empathy" and the notions of "reciprocity" or "respect" I have discussed stand for? Without reciprocity, for example, in a couple where love is not equal on each side, there is no *alter ego*. Even if I sacrifice myself for the other, Merleau-Ponty (1945: 409) reasons, it does not mean that I care about the other as much as I care about myself, since *I* am the one who decided to be altruistic. I have read *Nausea* just as I would have vomited—by accident. Yet reading *Nausea* was also serendipitous—Sartre expressed an all-too-familiar sensation with the fierceness that characterised my fieldwork beyond my power of description. A nauseous diary! At last a story resonated with my first experience of the field, like a novel with its brilliant on-screen adaptation. The melancholic hero of *Nausea* (Sartre had first given the title *Melancholia* to this book) feels he is "one too many" in the world, just as I felt superfluous in the advertising agency. As he is having lunch with a self-taught humanist, Roquentin casts his eye over the people in the restaurant and a violent disgust pulses through him:

> Why are these people here? Why are they eating? It's true they don't know they exist. I want to leave, go to some place where I will be really in my own niche, where I will fit in... But my place is nowhere; I am one too many. (Sartre, 1981: 144)

In a muffled scream of terror, Roquentin realises that however pointless or disgusting it is to exist, we all continue to do so without a proper reason or necessity. People invent lamentable "necessities" where there are none—a love for someone, an attachment to the family, to work, to possessions, etc. They make Roquentin sick. Roquentin lives alone, alone with his reflections, his inner self, and his own person makes him sick. A memorable passage of the mirror details the intensity of his crisis. Existence (whether of animals, rocks, plants, or people) is absurd:

> We were a heap of living creatures, irritated, embarrassed at ourselves, we hadn't the slightest reason to be there, none of us, each one, confused, vaguely alarmed, felt in the way in relation to the others. (Sartre, 1981: 152)

Fieldwork in an advertising agency

Abjection

What a sense of *déjà vu* these words stirred up! That was it, life in the advertising agency—this business gathered a heap of awkward beings. Clients embarrassed advertising people; advertising people embarrassed clients; they annoyed me; I annoyed them. And I did not feel like recording anything apart from the extraordinary wastes of time this business indulged in. I remember this waste! So many vain efforts and gratuitous meetings, so many silly gossips and chitchats... I think the Taiwanese have a word for people who puke their logorrhoea around: "scooters." They putt-putt. Finding myself in an open office with copywriters and art directors, I listened indolently to their jokes, which filled me with melancholia. At times I would even feel dizzy, caught in a whirlpool of giggles and not laughing myself, or physically sitting in front of a bulky Macintosh and spiritually brooding elsewhere, in some faraway dystopia. I was paralysed by my own contempt towards this team. I believed that anthropology was driven by a love for people, yet I could not help but despise them in silence. I hated myself for that. Was I ashamed of sharing their everyday work because it reflected the meaninglessness of my own life? I think this is what is called despair. I was not exactly a researcher, not exactly a copywriter and my place was "nowhere"; yet here I "was," by some operation of misfit or wrongness, among them. And what about them, who without questioning their own lives believed they were so important and charismatic? Surely they "didn't know they existed"! I would lose myself into a secret, solitary pride of knowing how absurd this all was, and contained the hysteric burst of laughter that would accuse it all.

Julia Kristeva (1980) would call my experience abjection, which refers to the rejection in the Other of things that I also find disgusting in myself. Before I see myself in the Other, before I break the narcissistic mirror and identify the Other as ob-ject of desire who makes me *be* (see also Lacan, 1977: 257–267), who becomes *alter ego*, I reject, ab-ject. Abjection is the first, genuine feeling of a subject in its formation as subject. This understanding of abjection is in many ways reassuring. Not just bad things happen when you begin to lose faith in your methods. It is okay to doubt. Knowledge surfaces from the wobbly edifice of a methodology in becoming and not from the deep-rooted foundations of certainty; from questions and not answers. So I preferred to remain in conflict with my methodology rather than revel in one of the narcissistic deliria I have quoted earlier in this book. For Sartre, who found himself ugly, the mirror was a problem, not a solution. I have a "love and hate" relationship to ethnography, and will remain sceptical as to what it may achieve.

Antoine Roquentin does not work, he writes. For him writing is not working, it is trying to be; whereas working is already knowing that we are. In the advertising agency I had nausea. What was his like? The first time, it occurred in the café he knows so well in Bouville:

> The Nausea is not inside me: I feel it out there in the wall, in the suspenders, everywhere around me. It makes itself one with the café, I am the one who is within it. (Sartre, 1981: 26)

At this moment nausea was wrapping him. It was the environment. But then this suffocating environment cut straight through him:

> The Nausea has not left me and I don't believe it will leave me so soon; but I no longer have to bear it, it is no longer an illness or a passing fit: it is I. (Sartre, 1981: 150)

Roquentin eventually resigned himself to it. *He* became the Nausea. As he no longer suffered from it, nausea had less to do with a disease than a lingering feeling of *ennui*, a disillusioned lassitude or indifference towards life. Kristeva (1980: 157) claims that such ennui characterises, along with abjection and "strident laughter," modernity.

Overdose

In the advertising agency I participated less and less in the activities of the group. My relations with managers and the marketing staff were exemplary, but with the creatives they quickly deteriorated. I gradually became the malaise that I had first discovered around me. Nausea in this agency was not just painted on these posters and computer screens, of a sickening triteness. It was in *me*. I was a nuisance, I was one too many. But what else could I say about this, without "forcing truth"? Was I expecting "something more" to write about? Were we not "too many" already? The creatives saw me as a freak. They liked to tease me, linking my behaviour to images of abnormality or deviance, to mental illnesses, and addictions to drugs. What was wrong with me, there was nothing wrong with me. We spoke different languages and our conversations typified only (and so much) miscommunication. We did not fit together. Perhaps I was insane among reasonable people, or else the only sane individual in a crazy environment. It was all the same. For who in our mad lives would locate where madness is? If nowadays a group of people developed a taste for crusades, they would be considered mentally ill. And so may posterity judge some of the ideas dominating our times. Since the creatives' irony would no longer surprise me after day one, I felt like a prisoner of my times, incapable of noticing the "strange" around me. *Too much* commonsense, I reckon this is what madness is about. It is about seeing life as it is, not as it could or should be, not as Don Quixote saw it. Don

Quixote would probably make a brilliant anthropologist, because he lives, like the artist, "in the triangle which remains after the angle which we may call common sense has been removed from this four-cornered world" (Soseki, 1968: 48).

As soon as anthropology attempts to make sense of people's lives, it sentences itself to a perilous paradox—these lives really "exist," while their rationalisation through writing does not. The revelation that life cannot be "explained" hits Roquentin as he stares at the root of some very ordinary tree in a key passage of his diary. He writes that:

> the world of explanations and reasons is not the world of existence. A circle is not absurd, it is clearly explained by the rotation of a straight segment around one of its extremities. But neither does a circle exist. This root, on the other hand, existed in such a way that I could not explain it. (Sartre 1981: 153)

My attempt at describing an advertising agency was in this way bound to be fragile, and probably sterile. These meetings, these posters, these jokes... everything was a root Roquentin could contemplate. They were, and that was all. The concepts I developed might "make sense," like circles, yet they did not "exist" like my informants' practices. With such concepts I claimed that I could explain what cannot be explained. The triteness I immersed myself in *made me* sick, and made me *sick*. I had become the sick.

"Ethnogastritis" refers to this self-diagnosed disease of subjectivity, which motivates the quest for its own cure through writing. Ethnogastritis shows that the enemy of ethnography is the ethnographer; that nausea is the mainspring of any process of integration; that such integration involves transgression; that hindrances, frustrations, discomfort in the presence of other people can and should be sublimated; that in the initial stage of miscommunication one can unearth the fecund roots of a methodological existentialism.

Contingency

In one of his notebooks Sartre situates ennui in the cohabitation of excess and scarcity:

> People are bored. Animals are bored. (...) What on earth is ennui? It is where there is not enough and too much at the same time. Not enough because there is too much, too much because there is not enough. (Sartre, 1981: 1684)

The note is perhaps better understood in conjunction with the preceding point about Roquentin not only feeling ennui, but also embodying it, like Emma Bovary (Flaubert, 2001). Madame Bovary leads an imaginary life through the fictions she reads. There is "not enough" out there in the real life to satisfy her; at the same time "too much" of her remains in this world she does not belong to. When Flaubert declared "Madame Bovary is *me*," he projected his own existential boredom into her. He sublimated in writing his feeling of *being* ennui. *Nausea* does not suggest that existence is horrible; it states that life is nothing more than life. In the advertising agency, I realised that advertising was just advertising; there was no mystery, no treasure to be found, no princess to set free from the forces of evil, no romance, no *adventure*. One evening Antoine Roquentin felt adventurous. How foolish he felt when he *awoke* the next day! Had he fallen into the trap of necessity? Much later in his diary, he is finally convinced—existence is not necessity. What matters is the refusal of necessity, it is *contingency*, because to exist is to be out there, nothing more, nothing less. Those who assume they have rights, who freeze themselves in a self-explanatory role, who posit their existence as necessary, are "Bastards" (Sartre, 1981: 155). The Bastards lie to themselves while Roquentin works on being true to himself. Roquentin represents truth.

The discovery of contingency as a guiding principle for us to really "exist" (and not just pretend to do so) inaugurates Sartre's philosophy of freedom. Biehl and Locke's (2010) "anthropology of becoming" adopt a Deleuzian approach that "illuminates desire and possibility." This anthropology seeks to portray people "whose actions are contingent" within a "constricted (...) universe of choices"; but in order to "bring alternatives within closer reach," as they say, the anthropologist may have no choice but to go through Roquentin's nauseous phase. This phase is to assess without populism or miserabilism whether or not people are true to themselves and, against determinisms, highlight contingencies. The anthropology of becoming also insists on a somewhat taken-for-granted "respect"; yet it does not question, envision, or prepare the possibility of respect. And if anthropologists are to foresee opportunities and change, they might as well "disrespect" the current state of affairs. The politics of anthropology does not just arise from listening to what people have to say, but also from dissatisfactions with what we are hearing. In this sense nausea can be seen, not as a negative relation to people, but as the positive building of their hopes.

Disintegration and miscommunication

Recurrence of ethnogastritis in other fields

Methodology is a response to the anxiety that the research situation elicits in the researcher (Agar, 1980: 42). In the advertising agency, people would mostly tell me what I wanted to hear, what I needed to do, and in the end I was not inscribing their lives but my own frustrations about the impossibility of my task. I eventually read my field notes through the lens of *Nausea* as a diary without any other end than itself; a journal for the sake of a journal; my bitter book of Lamentations. The methodological struggles identified earlier were linked to a model of "participant observation," which made integration both mandatory and prohibited. Integration conceived in this way is bound to fail, but still conditions anthropology and leads it straight to hell. As Garcin famously put it towards the end of one Sartre's (2000: 148) plays, "So this is what hell is like. (...) Do you remember brimstone, the stake, the gridiron?...What a joke! No need for the gridiron—Hell is other people." The phrase draws attention to the tension involved in imperatives of integration, of tolerating others. There is no escape—no escape from people, no escape from oneself. Closely articulated to this tension is that of *communication*, which I would like to explore now through personal experiences in the field.

Ethnogastritis is gastritis in the field affecting mind and body (especially in hot climates, for European and Anglo-Saxon ethnographers). It also refers to the pathology of fieldwork methods, notably issues that researchers tend to repress or disregard: what to do when I have to write about people I cannot understand or feel close to? While doing fieldwork in Western Africa (Mali, Sénégal, Burkina Faso), I witnessed behaviours that were so different from my own that I felt antipathy more often than populist excitement. Nauseous situations and miscommunications were not caused by one party. They were shared responsibilities that seemed oddly irremediable. We were different and that was that. I find the experience of inequality (of education, wealth, and everything that empowers) in the field virtually unbearable. This experience is probably worse for the poor than for the rich, even if Lévi-Strauss (1955: 135) writes, reflecting on his experience in Calcutta, that the poor do not want to be equal—they beg him to crush them with his arrogance, since the wider the gap between him and them, the more substantial the bribe they can expect.

I experienced the following event in Burkina Faso, which shows that the anthropologist is trapped between a colonial past and a touristic present; between the neo-colonial attitude of the expatriate, the humanistic pride of the populist activist, and the pathetic naivety of the holiday-maker (Michel, 2004: 264).

Burkina Faso, 2009

"Nassara! Pssst! Le blanc!," someone calls out as I walk by the crowded market.

I look around and have no clue where the voice came from. I do see, on the other hand, hundreds of eyes watching my every move. People walk past me and look back, others stare. I stride along the dusty street and my feet raise red ochre puffs, tiny little clouds.

"Nassara!," another voice shouts.

This time I notice a man standing on my left, smiling and gesturing for me to come over. I also catch a glimpse of the pair of shoes he is holding, which looks cheap and dreadful. Behind me, a muffled conversation—that of two strangers who have been shadowing me for some time, and are now catching up with me as I imperceptibly slow down to return a constricted smile to the shoe seller. I am not sure whether they want to sell me the wares they carry with them, or bring me to their shop via one of their rehearsed stratagems. Soon other stalkers seem to join them. Or am I getting paranoid? Paranoia is no anomaly in Ouagadougou, but the rule guiding the behaviour of the white. I am an attraction and "money" is written on my forehead. People scan me from head to toe. My body is covered with barcodes. Beep, beep, beep ... here is an expensive fellow, they must be thinking.

A little girl appears out of nowhere and hurries toward me. She wears rags, her skin is dusty and she indolently chases the flies zigzagging close to her or landing on her face. Before she opens her mouth I know what she is going to say:

"Gift?"

Her family must have taught her to beg from white people, who will be more inclined to pity young children. She joins the group of locals walking around me for a while. Someone shouts at her in Moré, probably telling her off. She runs ahead to face me and looks straight into my eyes. I am forced into glancing back at the desperate expression on her face as she whispers:

"There's no money."

She reaches out to touch my hand. I ignore her. She gives up, disappears. It is 3 pm and I must have been talking to fifty people already, mostly male adults (women by tradition prepare the food) selling all sorts of things, especially phone cards. Already overwhelmed by the afternoon heat, my head feels like an anvil hit by the hammers of their voices. It is extremely difficult in this district to avoid conversations, which systematically involve money and bargaining. "You must encourage me" is the stock phrase that concludes a standard discourse on the poverty of the artist and the authenticity of his work. Keeping calm, when every second I am asked to buy or donate, proves to be a challenge. I hear "my friend!" and intuitively quicken my pace, because I do not want to engage with them, because these are not human relationships but pressured, interest-driven interactions. Everyone wants to be "my friend."

And as I ignore these people every day, I pretend not to see what ties me to them, and my humanity gradually leaves my senses, sneaks out of my body. With every refusal, every "no, thank you" that I utter like an automaton or a drum machine, an inner tension builds up. Guilt is devouring me. I no longer know what is acceptable to think and do. To avoid being entirely consumed by the inhumanity that grows inside them, the whites take refuge in cynicism. They endorse a colonial attitude in response to the distress that the indigenous population simultaneously suffers and stages. I try to be kind and strict at the same time. I begin to give orders and hallucinate. Tragic masks loom menacingly around me:

"There's no money ..."

They are real mirages, they talk to me, they grasp my hand, they keep talking to me. They oppress me. Sometimes they spring to my face like jack-in-the-boxes:

"Gift?"

Could my own guilt feelings have taken on the form of nausea or made me hear things that were not there? One evening I sit on a wooden stool in a quiet street, sipping a Coke. I look up at a minaret bathing in the splendour of the sunset. And of the thought that enters my head at this instant I am almost immediately ashamed—tender is the night when I don't have to hear them; tender is the night that makes me look darker.

The next day I sit on a kerb in the city centre, pausing for thought and gulps of water.

"You must encourage me ..."

I can smell fruits. Flocks of children play noisily and happily, racing in and out of a shed. Inevitably after a couple of minutes, a seller comes to me. Before he even starts talking I snap "no." He shows me the usual motorcycle made of can and tin parts and iron threads, before delivering a speech that I punctuate with "nos." Staring into the void, I passively listen to half of his lament and understand he is Malian and does not want to get into delinquency like his mates. I endeavour not to pay him any attention but the restless flow disturbs my ears. I stand up and walk away but the seller follows me, this time giving his last shot—I don't need to buy his objects, but I can just give him whatever I want, even a small amount will do. At this point I look at him and say:

"But you've just told me you've never begged?"

As he realises he won't get anything from me, his tone suddenly changes. He points a threatening finger at me:

"You! You're just a bastard."

"Okay, well, bye now."

"You're a son of a bitch!"

His face expresses so much contempt, so much hatred. So I have just listened to a remarkable acting performance, when he spoke with polite softness only seconds before. He disappoints me, especially now that he vociferates:

"I've spent so much time with you, and you're giving me nothing in return ..."

"I told you 'no' ten times ..."

"Go burn in hell, all this is your fault, you colonised us, now you look down upon us ..."

The accusation sounds both fair and unfair, and makes me wonder whether I have to personally bear the weight of history, whether I have to feel responsible for the acts of my forefathers, whether I have moral and practical obligations towards the Burkinabè.

"There's no money ..."

Tricky—I never asked to be born into this world. He goes on with his ranting for a short while, then his voice fades away. I keep walking, but he is soon beside me again:

"You're a son of a bitch... a little son of a bitch"

"You're still here? Won't you go away? Far away please"

The violence of the episode reminds me of my schooldays. For a split second, I consider hitting the teenager, who does not look very strong, with my elbow. That would be cowardly but neat.

"You must encourage me."

But I also quickly picture the consequences of my act: Look at this white guy, hitting a kid! Shame on him! Who does he think he is? A little son of a bitch, that's what he is! So instead, I cross the street feigning indifference. The truth is, I am tense, but not completely upset. In the "Faso," as the French ambassador calls it, I have a clearer idea about who I am. I am the white monkey without organs, stuffed with banknotes. Surrounded by people who emphasise *my strangeness, my exceptionality, I cannot feel more out of place. You must encourage me, too.*

Despite the irrelevance of hate in therapeutic treatment, Winnicott (1958) stresses that psychiatrists must identify it and elaborate on it, so as to produce a response adapted to the needs of the patient and not to their own needs. In this way, care will seem to be given spontaneously, when in reality it is only given in response to the patient's needs. Hate which is felt, yet not recognised, results in guilt and shame. Shame, as outlined above, may in turn develop into for people and self-hatred, and so forth in a vicious circle. Although Winnicot's recommendation applies to relationships with psychotic patients, it offers important directions for anthropologists dealing with violent situations; besides, as hinted above, madness has long characterised colonial relationships. In the episode that took place in Burkina Faso, it was vital to recognise and face hate, not escape it. Successful management of this hate should make the Malian boy feel that my attitude is not self-interested but natural, and that I am more interested in caring for him than preserving myself (when the reality is different since I am containing my anger).

I hate the Malian beggar because he cheats me, betrays me, lies to me, and in the end disgusts me. The abject for Kristeva (1980: 12) is what disturbs an order, or disrespects the limits or the rules. It is the in-between, the ambiguous—the betrayer, the liar, the shameless criminal. This in-between is also reminiscent of the "liminal" position of the ethnographer "in the field but not of the field," the writer of "true fictions" who moves back and forth between participant and observer roles, now incorporating, now stepping outside the community (Jackson, 1995: 38). Hence this ethnographer discovers through the Other the abject that also exists inside her. Nevertheless, the ambiguity of the abject is not pure evil. Love and hate are close feelings—both are excesses of energy directed at the Other, consuming passions, desires to become "one" by fusion with, or annihilation of the Other (Bataille, 1957: 27). I would like to expand on this ambiguity taking the notion of communication as a starting point. In Burkina Faso my failure of integration, my "disintegration" appears in the impossibility of dialogue. It appears as language fails us. Such disintegration was foreseeable before the plane landed, because of a colonial history of domination based on racist tales of civilisation and genetic superiority. But even "at home," in my own culture where the majority is white, I may feel out of place.

United Kingdom, 2009

I like what Georg Simmel (cited in Benjamin, 1999: 38) says about public transportation. It causes a preponderance of the activity of the eye, in big cities, over that of the ear:

> Before the development of buses, railroads, and trams in the nineteenth century, people had never been in a position of having to look at one another for long minutes or even hours without speaking to one another.

Contemporary London is very much an Orwellian space of surveillance, particularly in the underground in which Big Brother's speakers, everywhere relaying cameras, tell commuters what to do and where to go. Inside the "tube" people face each other and yet ignore each other; a bizarre situation reproduced around the world.

I am sitting in the London tube somewhere on the Circle Line. Around me people read newspapers, listen to music in their headphones, text friends on their mobile phone, talk to their friend or partner... the usual underground scene. A charming couple sits opposite me. She is whispering in his ear, they are holding hands, they look beautiful and very much in love. Their happiness is contagious and I smile at them. But unexpectedly, she looks straight in my eyes and with an outraged expression on her face snarls: "What's so funny?"

Here is a simple example of misinterpretation... and we speak the same language! Words are not even required for this basic interaction to succeed, and it fails miserably. Communication is not a matter of language. The strongest emotions, such as the disgust I feel towards the two-faced Malian boy and the quick-tempered London girl are experienced on the spot, directly through the senses and not through reason, and as such hardly describable in writing. In addition, emotions are not innate but to a great extent taught, inherited from the environment in which the individual grew up. Misunderstandings and miscommunications therefore develop from a lack of cultural knowledge (first reflected in either ignorance of, or limited fluency in the other's language). The insufficient knowledge available for the individual to fill this gap, commonly called "stereotypes," shape parochialisms, ethnocentrisms, and eventually the reactions of rejection called "xenophobia." Misread emotions maintain the spiral of violence between cultures. Foreign perceptions of Japan offer perfect illustrations, particularly "what's-so-funny" episodes, of this process. Thus at the end of the 19th century, Pierre Loti (1925a, 1925b) finds Japanese things and people so risible that he can neither repress his giggles nor his disdain. He believes the Japanese laugh for no reason, and laughs at them. And his lyrical racism makes for stunning literature! Lafcadio Hearn (2007: 657) contrasts the "angry faces" of foreigners, as seen by the Japanese, and the "Japanese smile" that for foreigners betrays insincerity. In reality, the Japanese smile does not always signify amusement or pleasure. A silent language of propriety as part of a social obligation (*giri*), it may communicate embarrassment and even grief (Clapier-Valladon, 1991: 259). Hearn (2007: 660, 669) suggests that laughter can be interpreted as "politeness carried to the utmost point of self-abnegation," which sheds light on the anecdote of the maid who, "smiling as if something very pleasant had happened," asks her mistress permission to attend her husband's funeral. She returns in the evening and, showing the little urn that contains the husband's ashes, says with a laugh: "That is my husband." Today there is an enduring belief among westerners that Japanese humour does not really exist or that the Japanese take everything literally (Okada, 2012: 180; Pons, 2012).

To understand emotions (anger, love, guilt, and so on) as universal and transferrable is a serious mistake, which ethnocentrically assumes that different cultures share the same system of meanings (Le Breton, 2001: 126). Emotions confuse and mislead us, triggering the clashes and passions that are most meaningful to ethnography. While the most complete or satisfying form of communication may be contained in the laughter of two persons sharing a joke (and what best reflects culture, to my mind, is people's sense of humour), the reverse is also true—miscommunication is most blatant when one regards as funny and trivial what the other thinks is shocking and serious. Oddly enough, culture is first and foremost language, but a language does not signify a culture. If language does not necessarily implies communication or culture, what does? I suggest that communication and integration are perhaps best understood through the unspeakable and incommunicable—through eroticism.

Eroticism

No images

Kulick and Willson's (1995) collection touches upon the fundamental issue of communication and relationship building; but it confuses sex and eroticism, even using the terms as substitutes. For example, Killick (1995: 76) pinpoints a "homology between ethnographic knowledge and carnal knowledge" and Altork (1995: 111–112) deplores the permanence of the mind-body split inherited from Western medical science, which anaesthetises "our own erotic and sensual responses"; but like most contributors, they refer to sexual temptations and relations in the field, that is, to the most boring urges of mating and copulation. As they wonder whether it is ethical to have sex with natives, they obliterate the emotions of a more ambivalent experience of the other. The religious layer that Goulet and Miller's (2007) edited volume superposes to Fabian's (2000) discussion of *ecstasis* is not my cup of tea either, even if some illustrations are worth mentioning. Gardner (2007: 22, 24) notes, for instance, that alcohol may enhance communication. He learns to play this game whereby one is allowed to claim amnesia for what was said and done in an intoxicated state the day before. Wilkes (2007: 82) recounts her own ecstasis at the "Sundances": "the relentless prairie sun burning [her] skin, the physical pain of long hours dancing, singing, and sweating under those conditions"; and the pleasures of friendship and joint prayers.

More insightful are Malinowski's diaries, filled with accounts of erotic fantasies and longings that afflicted him in the course of fieldwork. The way in which Rabinow (1977: 63, 65–67) writes of his excursion with Ali and four girls also deserves attention, because his writing is "crippled" by innuendos revealing his reticence to fully communicate his intimate feelings to the reader. After arousing our curiosity ("I had never before had this kind of sensual interaction in Morocco"), he leaves us with work-it-out-for-yourself euphemisms ("the air became purer and the play freer. Both Ali and the Berber girls let me be, not shunning me but not pushing either, leaving the definition of my limits up to me"). Why is such an important experience made invisible? As they reach a memorable hot spring in the mountains, Rabinow's ethnography becomes more evocative and rather remarkable. But even then, the modesty he describes in his swimming companions applies to his writing: "Images of the baths in Sefrou rushed through my mind as I sat watching them." The reader might want to know more about his daydreams. These images matter. Rabinow was not just "too timid" to go swimming himself, but I daresay timid enough to censor his own thoughts and preventing them from reaching us. Eroticism is never dependent on the explicit and the crude in writing, but must at least elaborate on emotions, and communication between people.

Somewhere, 2013

In the plane bound for Taipei, I read a detective novel that takes place in Taipei: "No woman in the world can remain as silent as the Chinese lady, who is dumb as an oyster when she has decided she is not interested in you" (Kenny, 1995: 113). I look towards the aisle. The flight attendant is as gorgeous and silent as a statue! I dream of possessing her, of capturing her like a wild animal, in an air safari, and display her as trophy back home. Am I any better than the idiot engaging in sexual tourism? Crazy me! Love and hate converge in such craziness. Passions are not discursive. The main characters in celebrated films of Wong Kar-wai or Kim Ki-duk hardly say a word, and the emotional beauty of their works is entrancing. In Wong's Chungking Express, *Tony Leung Chiu-Wai even manages to date a flight attendant. I leave the book and think about which film I should watch. The flight attendant has just given us a drink. Talk to me, creature of the unknown! Reveal yourself to me, let me touch and smell and taste you, and swallow you, and keep you in my body, so you become a part of me and I have all the time in the world to know you, and love you.*

Another cannibalistic daydream! For Sartre, existentialism is humanism. For Segalen (1978: 72), exoticism is eroticism. He writes that the young girl (and he means virgin) is the true lover because she is extremely distant from him. Only supreme otherness may "inspire the deepest love, and the most powerful desire for knowledge."

If the things we do not want to come out eventually come out, we have difficulties accepting them. Via some defence mechanism they become illusions, hallucinations. Thus guilt feelings made Murakami's friend "hear things that were not there"; Rabinow refused to inscribe (to share) "images" in his memory, as if his real past was just a dream. Anthropologists tend to misdiagnose ethnogastritis, from which no one is immune, and on which their research could even be based, because they mistake a disease for a cure—thus reflexivity and respect become ready-made foils, methodological fetishes. Instead, ethnogastritis reconsiders the unfairness, the cruelty, the revulsion of the Self towards the Other. And as long as it is properly treated, the malady yields its remedy; it draws its strength from the recognition that the Self always behaves "selfishly" or "self-centredly" in its struggle to accept and represent the Other. I am not sure Antoine Roquentin makes this connection in his diary, but it occurred to me that nausea itself expressed a contingency; not irremediable vomiting but a risk that it might occur. For an anthropology of becoming to be feasible, we must discover this contingency in ourselves and in others. Again I must take the liberty, for purposes of illustration, to refer to my own experience—one of the earliest episodes of my life, incidentally, I can recollect. With apologies for the intensity of abjection it contains! But ethnography is literature, and literature shows no mercy.

France, *circa* 1983

When I woke up this morning I first saw the cot's wooden bars that prevent me from falling if I toss about in my sleep. They were painted in white, and they did not make me feel very safe. I also felt that my face was soaked in something. And I could smell an acrid odour—not an unpleasant odour, just one I could not quite identify. My eyes were only half-open but I recognised some apple compote. What was it doing here? Then I must have dozed off since I instantly found myself in the dining room on my baby chair. In this dream, I looked with disgust at the compote in the plate in front of me. It was a sweet puree I was fond of, but with dodgy bits in it. It was contaminated! I refused to eat it. My dad scolded me: "These are bits of apple! It's an apple!" And I was forced to swallow the compote, reluctantly munching on the bigger bits. It was their texture that felt unpleasant, not their taste. This really happened a few days earlier, my brain was just playing back the scene. It is with horror, later, that I realised I had tasted the vomit my cheeks and pillow were covered with.

In this episode the boundaries between dream and reality are not clear-cut. A fiction, a dream-reality, affects my relation to reality. A premonition makes sense. This is the first erotic experience—I find the sweetness desirable but also tantalizing, and feel unable to "cross the line" and push the experience further (down the throat). So I made a connection between my very first pleasures (jars of baby food) and my first revulsions (vomiting). It was the very same object that caused my eating with delight and my rejecting with pain. The joy I had in ingesting delicious baby food was never safe from the terror of rejecting it. There was always this disturbing likelihood, in pleasurable sensations, of a nausea that frightened me. I began to understand nausea as evidence that dainties, sex, and all distractions contained an insidious poison that punished the pleasure seeker. As if there was a price to pay for everything we desired. Nausea is the manifestation of dormant threats lurking in our desires. Repulsions are embedded in our attractions; excesses in our normal behaviours; laughter in our seriousness.

I have been for many years (albeit neither too seriously nor traumatically) emetophobe. Later I turned emetophile, which at first sight might appear as a bizarre reversal; however, the repulsion/attraction convergences that psychoanalysis highlights convinced me that my phobia simply gave way to their latent erotic content. What disgusts us also fascinates us; what disturbs us also arouses us. As young children, what causes our eating with delight and our rejecting with pain is not so different—delicious food here, and there the ignominious gastric fluids those delicacies became. As teenagers some of us identify the same ambiguities in alcohol—friend and foe, integrator and disintegrator towards the most humiliating degradations. From drugs to the thrills of "risky" behaviours and other death drives, the very good things that fulfil us are simultaneously the very bad things that destroy us. Thus the orgies of the Roman Empire are said to accelerate its "decadence." The pursuit of pleasure always contains this *likelihood* of overconsumption, of excess, of nausea—dramatic spurting of bodily fluids; incontrollable secretions, leaks, drips, and streams that accompany the spasms of agony and the explosion of orgasm (whose splendour universally compares with fireworks); and of course terrifying visions and smells of our materiality, and abject sputters and excretions that summon up animality, rot, and death. Our desires are not for fulfilment but for more desire, more of this risk that we are willing to take. The temptation of the abject makes sense: so ecstatic the experience, so liberating the purge!

Managing excess

Nausea carries a "potential energy," as physics would call it, which announces deliverance, release, relief, appeasement. Soothing of a tension, calm after the storm. Vomiting may be more positive than meets the eye, as a way of getting rid of unpleasant or harmful things and people, as a form of purification or even atonement. Expectant mothers who experience nausea for longer than is usual are even told of a happy omen—extensive sickness would indicate that the baby is more strongly rooted in the mother and less likely to come to harm during pregnancy. Whether this omen has scientific resonance or a mythical function designed to comfort women, it gives a glimpse of how nausea may be experienced as a constructive and transformative process. In consequence ethnogastritis refers to the creative violence through which excess (we are too many) and ennui (we are meaningless) are managed. Sartre concentrates on the initial frustrations and feelings of wrongness or unfairness that motivate such management. For example, Roquentin's first nausea is triggered by a sexual frustration as he cannot "fuck" the barmaid. The metaphor of the obscene underlies the hero's ruminations about contingency. For Sartre (1981: 1785) the obscene has to do with feminine "passivity," with over-sexualised women. It is found in the soft, the sticky, the glutinous. Roquentin writes:

> All things, gently, tenderly, were letting themselves drift into existence like those relaxed women who burst out laughing and say: "It's good to laugh," in a wet voice; they were parading, one in front of the other, exchanging abject secrets about their existence. (Sartre, 1981: 151)

Nausea is sometimes portrayed as dizziness before a feminised world, fear and simultaneously temptation to give into one's urges, to swoon for pleasure and open oneself like the spongy "mussel"—female genitals in French slang.

The works of Georges Bataille (1970, 1973a, 1973b, 1976) explore the management of excess in more depth. The erotic imagery Bataille unrolls is in the same way flabby, gluey, replete with slimy associations such as "eyes" and "eggs" (caused by an upsetting event in his childhood and phonetic similarities between these words in French), with gushes and flows of life, with various taboos. And yet the philosopher insists, referring to erstwhile rituals, on positive uses of excess. People always produce more than the strict minimum they require, but the erotic energy of the resulting surplus is no longer understood—it has become an "accursed share." With capitalism, a "notion of spending" (the necessary dispersion, evacuation, release of accumulated energy) has vanished. People used to reach a state of "glory" through spending, losing, and squandering things and people in a burst of laughter. In Europe they died building cathedrals, and in North America the pride acquired in displaying wealth was inferior to that of its sudden destruction. In Indian ceremonies of the potlatch, in Maya sacrifices during which a heart was pulled out and brandished as it was still pulsating with life, humans were disposable. Spending was a glorious act, in that it reflected incredible capacities for generating wealth and at the same time posited that it was absurd to take life itself too seriously.

Sacrifice

In its broadest sense the *sacrifice* has therefore a vital function of transgression, visible through abject acts and relations of humiliations, which entail more or less radical destructions of the sacred, the extremely valuable (from material luxuries to animal and human lives, in the potlatch and other rituals of torture and execution). To this day humiliation remains a pillar of Japanese eroticism, and that makes it the most powerful and imaginative in the world. The unfair, the unjust, the disgusting captivates and is exalted in the spectacle. Giard (2007: 75) briefly recounts a vomit show at a "fetish" night in Tokyo, but misinterprets it as a cultural specificity, as an oddity. Eroticism explores the suggestive power of the abject; it reveals without further ado the logic of transgression (i.e., the intensification of desire linked to prohibitions) epitomised in the works of Sade (1990, 1995, 1998) and Bataille (1970, 1957). Eroticism occurs with the depravation of the beautiful, when innocence is perverted, when purity is soiled. Sade in his cell used to order the most delicate roses so as to pull off their petals above a manure pit.

Eroticism emanates out of ambivalence, of indecisiveness—for example, when the same person (especially the young and naïve type) commits the worst ignominies or suffers the worst humiliations. The erotic aspects of the *corrida* (bullfighting) that fascinates Bataille are echoed in Ōshima's *Realm of the Senses/Ai no Korīda*," literally "bullfight of love," which retells the obsession of Abe Sada for her lover's penis. It is never "natural beauty" that seduces, but "ritualistic beauty" (Baudrillard, 1979: 125). The sharp objects (blades, bull's horns, teeth, etc.) of death rituals (from the guillotine to bullfighting to the staged *seppuku* of Sadayakko) enable erotic transgression. If I say that the eye "sees," I imply that it produces images, that it "imagines" (Bachelard, 1957: 16–17), and at once underline its erotic faculty. Eroticism puts the eye to the test. In the shivers of rituals, it plays with what the eye "can take." No wonder eyes have become erotic objects in bloody ceremonies (Freud, 1962: 99) and surrealist works—a human eye is gouged out in Bataille's (1970) *Story of the Eye*, gashed in Buñuel and Dalí's *Un Chien Andalou*. Only such impossible situations, only literature may reveal the true nature of the erotic (Bataille, 1973a: 152).

Inner experience

So Jean-Paul Sartre discovers contingency through nausea, and it appears that nausea itself is an erotically charged contingency. Bataille (1973b) makes an important distinction between "discursive knowledge" and the "inner experience." The inner experience is a purely emotional form of meditation accessible through acts of "spending" (laughter, poetry, sacrifice, ecstasy, eroticism, etc.). These communicative acts constitute a *non-knowledge* that is never reachable through texts but through direct experience. The inner experience is opposed to action (thinking, speaking, etc.) because action amounts to planning, to postponing existence to the future, to being dead in the present. It is worth noting in passing that such meditation may be construed in the spirit of Taoism. Both Lao Tzu and Chuang Tzu have rejected discursive science and suggested that true knowledge is of an ecstatic order accessible through trance—a voyage "at the origins of all things" that compares with shamanic mysticism (e.g., Eliade, 1992: 35). While phenomenology is concerned with how experience leads to knowledge as an end in itself, Bataille's inner experience does not reveal anything and has no other end than itself—it only questions, in some feverish torment, what one knows about being.

The inner experience often appears in Bataille's works as intense forms of communication and empathy, with some extreme (sur-realist) experience of the other, such as sacrifices, cases of dementia involving mutilation and self-harm (Van Gogh's ear, this Gaston F. who bit off and ate his own finger), or excruciating practices of North-American tribes or pre-Colombian civilisations that sought to communicate with the other world (see also Mircea Eliade's (1992, 1989a: 29, 286, 322, 1989b: 18, 35) breathtaking treatises on shamanism). To sacrifice oneself, or part of oneself, is to identify with the victim, to throw oneself out of oneself, to "vomit one's own being" (Bataille, 1970: 269). Sacrifices and erotic rituals enhance the cohesion of a group in the face of the horror that equally terrorises and fascinates them. They dramatise human fears and desires in order to play down their importance, their seriousness. We best communicate and feel closest to each other when we witness death before our eyes, whether in its actual or represented form. The experience that we share moves us and unites us beyond discourse. Such experience (sexual arousal, or dreadful shiver running through our bodies when witnessing violence) is not usually accepted as knowledge. Instead, law, religion, and science construct the morality that channels our energy and restricts our murderous and sexual impulses. At the same time, the respect we have for morality reflects our fear of the non-validity of such rules—fear of a likelihood, fear of contingency.

The most sincere words appear from physiological rather than intellectual reactions to our surroundings. "What allowed me to step forward and talk," as Bataille (1976: 530) has it, "is less having read than having lived." I sense that this is exactly how fieldwork should be viewed—as an inner experience that surfaces "outside" knowledge, outside discourse. It is through a "cessation of all intellectual operation" (Bataille, 1973b: 25) that our mind is laid bare. Of course it will be difficult for anthropology to produce knowledge away from anthropological texts, that is, outside itself. People rely on discourse like pets on people. Yet anthropologists could try and unshackle themselves from words, concede that words will not allow them to "know," that no language game, no verbal trick may ever convey what we feel when the scent of a flower or the roar of a storm wakens a memory that so profoundly moves us. I see in nausea this eroticism, non-knowledge that could outdo the knowledge delivered in a "concept" or "explanation" of a cultural phenomenon. In this line of thought, anthropology would not be driven by adult "understanding" of an event through tropes, analogies, and myths in Geertz's (2000: 23) tradition; but by the exhilarations of the child "living through" the event without seeking any meaning out of it, or by the anxiety of the child transgressing a prohibition. Such anxiety, epitomised in the sacrifice, unites people and shows the path to communication. Anthropological writing can be empowered if it reads like a hysteric burst of laughter (but not the Sartrian giggles), like vertigo, and like poetry, which according to Bataille (1973b: 156) is the "sacrifice whose victims are words." The ambivalence and liminality of ethnographic methods situate the anthropologist between life and death, on the narrow ledge of eroticism. Truly erotic methods will place the anthropologist in front of the dizzying emptiness that will allow her to produce a vertiginous account. At the margin between familiarity and strangeness, the researcher takes on the ambiguity of the character played by Kim Novak in Hitchcock's *Vertigo*. Freud (1991: 375) associates vertigo to sexual desire, as well as Hitchcock who includes in background shots the "Coit Tower" as a phallic symbol communicating desire... not for the phallus itself, but for the Other (Lacan, 1977: 288). In the short passage below, I attempt to write something of the eroticism of vertigo.

France, 1990

In the beginning was the Diary. Yes! I began writing one in my teenage years... but I must have filled no more than five pages. I remember describing my feelings as my brother and I were sitting on a chairlift. In this upper section of the resort it was snowing and so foggy we could not see the structure that moved us. Suspended in the air, wrapped in the mists of the mountain, we were floating in nothingness, in some cotton-wool unreality. The freezing wind, the fear of falling sent shivers down my spine. But for the first time I also experienced the voluptuous delight of vertigo. I saw death so near, just beneath my skis. Their weight drew me downwards, as if death was pulling at my legs to make me fall. Tingling sensation of letting nature tease me, hint at my fate, pull my leg! My life hung only by a cable, which gently rocked us up and down. It felt so light, so serene in the white silence. Only the noise of the pulleys above us, when we approached a pylon, connected us to reality. It sounded like rubber bands being chewed, and I remember their unique timbre and the transient fright that came over me as it grew louder. We were going to find ourselves into someone's mouth and listen to the metronomic regularity of her mastication; or the sheaves were going to slice the cable and we would fall like rotten fruits off a tree. And I had this repressed desire to jump and touch the snow. Or I imagined myself standing on the last rung of one of the ladders attached to pylons, clutching the cold cylinder, gripped by panic, but slowly and irresistibly releasing my fingers until I fell backwards. The vision of my body smoothly landing and sinking in the powdery snow was chased away by another vision of its bouncing and breaking on the ice, or shattering against a rock. My blood would gush out, drawing dark red streams all around me. It would be so garish on the snow. It would be me down there, colouring millions of glittering crystals in just a few seconds. It would be me, this starfish of a disturbing beauty. Above, the little death of speechless skiers witnessing my stellar death!

Emotional writing

Julia Kristeva (1980) argues that abjection recognises the lack at the root of every being, every desire, every language. She insists on the fundamental incompleteness of words, of the symbolic. When a writer attempts to endow a text with the spontaneity and obscenity of the oral style, to capture emotion through a distortion of syntax and lexicon, she breaches "the ultimate guarantee of humanity that is language" and embraces instead the "inhumanity of the poet." Kristeva mentions Artaud, Kafka, Baudelaire, Lautréamont, Sade, Bataille, Céline, Sartre, and their representations of horror, death, insanity, war, orgy, crime, repugnance, dread, and the like. Anthropology has much to learn from literature. Take Céline's style, which aims to transfer the spoken into the written, to destabilise grammar, and restore the oral character of emotion. In the words of Céline (quoted in Kristeva, 1980: 222):

> You know, in the Scriptures it says, "In the beginning was the word." No! In the beginning was emotion. The Word came later, replacing emotion like trot replaced gallop, while the natural law of the horse is gallop; it is forced to break into trot. Man was removed from emotional poetry and pushed into dialectics, in other words, splattering, isn't that so?

Abjection as inner experience shows us the path to an anthropology through emotions, not language. In the poetic distortion of language, in its very refutation, anthropologists can escape the structure of conventional narration. They can splash the chaos of a dream, of a sensation, onto paper. Meaningful anthropology stems from messy ejaculations of ink in the field (field notes), not clean sentences typed in the comfort of an office. The bare crudeness of the scream, of the laugh, of the moan, can be exclaimed and flung at the reader; the whisper or the gasp, suspended. In the literature of Céline and Lautréamont, the exclamation mark conveys a horrified fascination with death, pain, idiocy, decay, violence, obscenity, and the overall animality of humanity. Ellipsis is hopelessness for such animality.

In the "what's-so-funny" examples above, a simple smile or a laugh is enough to trigger passions such as hatred. Literature, cinema, fantasies assuage our voyeuristic hunger for the tragic and the gore. We are horrified, both by what we see and by the pleasure we secretly take in seeing it. In other words we are ashamed and scared of our true nature, and for this reason exhibit it and play down its terror. A clown, for example, is this mirror that overturns shame by making it funny (Ciccone and Ferrant, 2009: 223). Her behaviour is at once distinguishable from the socially acceptable behaviours of "real" people who do not clown around. Laughter expresses in this way an awareness of the gap between what "should be" and what actually is. It results from surprise—a rupture from expectations, and between the real and the unreal. Young children seeing the clown in a circus perceive a more serious rupture than adults, who might need to reassure them that this is not "for real." When children ask, "Is he really dead?," they are really anxious about death. The feelings that fantasies (such as fairytales and staged performances) instil in us are very real (Bettelheim, 1976: 126). In *The Circus*, Chaplin is forced into tightrope walking. Without funambulist experience, his life ironically hangs by a thread, and laughing spectators believe they are seeing a comic performance. Further, what makes us laugh is precisely the fact that spectators ought not to laugh. The uncontrollability of laughter is therefore mysterious and frightening. This brilliant scene sustains tensions between acting and being, comedy and tragedy. Bataille (1970, 1976: 274–279) powerfully shows that laughter communicates the relief of an anxiety. What makes us laugh is the real, the substance of things, the undressed, and at last knowable nature.

Writing ethnogastritis

True communication functions like eroticism, and ambivalence is written all over eroticism. Stewart (2007: 27) captures an ambivalent feeling of being in the crowd for example, a "sense of shock or relief at being 'in' something with others. A weirdly floating 'we' snaps into a blurry focus when one enters a mall." The shopping mall is an example of "other space," a sort of "counter-space" that, like the island, defines itself in opposition to its surroundings (a concept I briefly mentioned above). But the archetype of the other space for Foucault (1994a, 2004) is the ship. Relationships on a ship, during the "other time" of the cruise holiday for example, exude eroticism. The ship sways, rocks people up and down; on the unstable deck their laughs and fears pitch and roll in time with the ship; they stumble and cling to each other; they sometimes fall together, or on each other, and with embarrassed hugs look deep into each other's eyes. Serge Gainsbourg composed a song entitled "love on the beat," which begins with the marine metaphor of eroticism and therefore, in some ways, love on the boat: "First I want to pick up thoughts in your mind with my (native) tongue, but you are already swinging your hips in the ebb and flow of tides." The ship is this very special place of ethnogastritis—a place where one feels simultaneously isolated and captive of one another; a place where hell is other people, and other people are us; a place filled with the eroticism of abjection and nausea. Céline (1981: 611) describes a scene of appalling nausea in *Death on Credit*:

> One passenger begs for mercy...He cries out to high heaven that he's empty...He strains his guts...And a raspberry comes up after all!...He examines it, goggle-eyed with horror...Now he really has nothing left!...He wishes he could vomit out his two eyes...He tries, he tries hard...He braces himself against the mast...he's trying to drive them out of their sockets...Mama collapses against the rail...She vomits herself up again, all she's got...A carrot comes up...a piece of fat...and the whole tail of a mullet.

Once again Céline "vomits inside the reader's mind" and holds up a mirror in which she can see herself (Ciccone and Ferrant, 2009: 136–137). Onboard the ship, passengers are vulnerable to the whims of *nature*, and human *nature* is laid bare. Onboard the ship, there is much anthropological truth to be found. I would like to recount a dreadful trip during which I saw reality with new eyes, with unhealthy eyes that are no longer afraid of death, and for this reason understand "healthy" life from the outside, from *above*, from an almighty and hysterical position of the non-living, of the living-dead. Reader! Skip the following passage if you have just eaten! It is disgusting! Stomach-churning! I wonder... I wonder who might find it hilarious... disgraceful... who could be turned on... off... upside down... whether this writing achieves anything... whether writing is always meant to communicate... Oops, oops, what is the matter with me? "You must encourage me ..." Reader! Just skip it no matter what! Tell me, will you be tempted to read it just because I order you to skip it?

Greece, 2007

For the first time in my life breathing is not quite automatic, and I concentrate on it. Never before have I paid so much attention to my heartbeat, pumping oxygen to all extremities of my body. I picture blood flooding through my swollen veins and I feel so liquid... Every now and then, sea spray whips my face. Dripping with salty water, my pathetic face... and my crumpled fingers, there, both hands have wrinkled up. They are as white as a cadaver's. The pain is unbelievable. I am rotting from the inside, and liquefying. My brain is rotating and grating against my skull, I am falling headfirst from the sky. The seasickness I experienced before was a trifling sting compared to this agony. I am sitting on the deck of a boat between the islands of Koufonissia and Amorgos. I heard that the force of the wind is 7 on the Beaufort scale, the upper limit for this nutshell to be authorised to navigate. A heavier ship could break those waves, flout their power; but this is no ship, and defenceless it espouses the every curve, the every jolt, the every bump of the undulating landscape. I am on a death boat shaken in all directions (even as I write this now, I come to doubt the stability of the ground). The journey should last a little more than three hours but time has evaporated. I hover in eternity. Visibility is poor but I can still make out, beyond the moist filter of the sky that hazes over, the blue-grey sea. Panting, I gaze ahead at this drenched backdrop while my insides jump with its hiccups. The unruly horizon bends. I look up above and the starry sky whirls. On this deck humans are staggering shadows, contorted automatons. No way! We are such uncanny creatures. I hear noises behind me. Unearthly noises! With considerable effort I turn around, at once feeling dizzier. Vision of a woman throwing up, her neck jerking and pecking like the chicken's, and now, splash! She vomits the sea. Her acrid projectiles have studded an ignominious plastic bag. She has come out of herself! Her lips have opened into a dysfunctional tap from which yellowish gushes, broken by yelps and sonorous growls, sluice out the inside surface of the bag. She has wetted her cotton top in the messy way a waterfall splatters rocks. The shirt has become a translucent rag that sticks to her skin, and reveals nipples hardened by the cold drizzle and her own tepid sick. Her legs are wobbling. She is no longer in this world. Gone! Melting before my eyes, vanishing in the anonymity of the night. From nowhere, a scream reaches my ears:

"Downstairs! Everybody downstairs!"

The voice was muffled by the whistles of the wind and the slaps of the swell against the hull. I take a glance around me. Few people remain on the upper deck. They have plastic bags with them, improvised sick bags. It might be raining, impossible to say... I already feel liquid anyway. As liquid and putrid as the vomit the woman continues to splutter behind me. Am I in perfect communion with nature at this instant? The weather and I have fused. I sense its brutality inside me. If I am dying for real, my body could be thrown overboard, sink to the bottom of the sea and become water, sand, and dust. I would turn into the nature that is wrapping me. The waves are so alive. Why am I stuck here? Shut up, sea! Let me think it over. Again I hear voices in the distance:

"Downstairs... is... etter! A... you... ing?"

"What did you say?," a man inquires.

"Are you coming?"

"I... eeda... ater... wait!"

I look back and now a couple sits behind. They are quiet; or perhaps very loud, but nature silences them. I feel a little cold but I could not care less. I understand it is recommended to come down to the lower deck however, so I stand up and head towards the stairs. After a few steps my nausea worsens. I reassure myself—things must be different downstairs. Better world, here I come. I now zigzag here and there, clutching backseats and iron bars and whatever I can hold on to. The floor suddenly tilts to the left, my arm hits something metallic and I almost fall down. A wave hits the hull and splashes over my shorts. Nearer the staircase I slip on a puddle but manage to dash to the wall of the cabin, avoiding another fall. Eventually I find myself at the entrance of the cabin. The place looks crowded as I take a peek inside. I get in.

I will never forget the nightmarish scene that I witness and perform in. I feel like the art student of Kurosawa's *Dreams*, who takes a journey inside Van Gogh's paintings. I have left the real world. I make my way along a very different *artwork however, not Van Gogh's fields but Géricault's Raft of the Medusa. Most people, in formidable postures of misery, bury their face in their hands. Some cower on their plastic chairs; others are slumped over tables, their eyes closed as if awaiting execution; over there people have lied down on couches and either suffocate as if rabid-stricken, or remain as motionless as corpses; a large group lay on the floor like breathing garbage on a wasteland. In this group a mother, with her legs folded, hugs her ghastly daughter whose long hair bathe in the dirt of the carpet. Children are weeping, women are moaning, men are grunting. I am mesmerized by the cacophony into which these startled beasts together burst. It is the sound of hell that rocks this boat! And we all go up, right, down, left, gasping at the ridge of a wave and blubbering down its hollow. Punctuating or covering the lamentations, the eructations and gurgles of nausea. What a circus! There, decadence! People contaminate each other and fill the already fetid air with yet more stench, as if it could be worse! Condensation has built up on the windows, cutting us off from the outside, locking us up in the rot of death and the excess of life. The air is hardly breathable but I do not feel capable of moving back to the upper deck. So I sit on a couch and force myself to stare at the spectacle in front of me, without fearing the release that might also strike me. At this moment I feel close to them, and at the same time shameful of our condition, of our vulnerability, of our grotesque lives. I share their pain, but they also make me sick. I love them, and I hate to be like them. This communion of a species that strives to exist with dignity moves me in many ways—it looks more complete, more definite, truer than any discourse on "human nature," or "culture." Here we are, here is our humanity, undressed in the epidemic that ravages us and unites us. The nearer we draw to death on this boat, the more alive we feel. There is so much of us in the abject.*

At some point I return to the upper deck, with no sense of time, for time has vanished long ago. Sitting on my plastic chair, I wish I died. I really do. Death would bring my seasickness to a close. The brownish bile I am now spitting irritates my throat. As I am pondering a desperate jump in the sea, I make out lights on the coast. We are approaching. Later I set foot on Amorgos, and watch my companions of misfortune disembark too. Oh, up there! A blonde woman is on the verge of collapsing. Her face has the colour of the moon, and the tears running down her cheeks glisten under the stars. Absolutely dazzling is the iciness of death she radiates.

Ethnogastritis is the opportunity to build on such mixed feelings, on abjection, on a transition from the horror of nausea on a boat (or that of a sacrifice) to the erotic energy that they communicate. Thus miscommunication, disintegration, and hatred in the advertising agency, in Burkina Faso, or the London tube are accepted as transitory but compulsory stages towards communication, integration, and love—points of relief when we all reach an understanding. Misery and despair are not our fate but enable the possibility of reversibility, of catharsis, just as death enables rebirth. Death is in this way a guiding principle of aesthetic emotion (Boltanski, 2007: 424). "The death, then, of a beautiful woman," Edgar Allan Poe (1846: 163) writes, "is, unquestionably, the most poetical topic in the world." A great number of artistic productions could demonstrate just that—what springs to my mind right now is Japanese, Korean, and French cinema, or J. G. Ballard's *Crash*, which sketches self-destruction in eroticism. There must be a dash of death in anthropological research, simply because it explores lives and sheds light on their creativity. Even the remote possibility of death spices up adventure, as Jankélévitch notes, and "makes it adventurous" (cited in Michel, 2004: 211). As a result, the "reflexivity" I have referred to earlier in the book must come close to Baudelairian reflexivity. The aesthetic goal of Baudelaire, who admired Sade, was to represent "both object and subject, the external world and the artist himself" (quoted in Boltanski, 2007: 220). The anthropologist must embody the "dandy" who gazes at her own gaze and faces violence in its simple truth—as pure evil. This reflexivity unveils the evil in the spectator herself and, as such, works towards abolishing the distinction between objectivity and subjectivity. Through a last example of ethnogastritis, below, I will reiterate that the communication that matters does not operate through words. Ethnogastritis, besides, does not exclusively deal with the abject and the tragic. It can be belch, not vomit; cough, not agony. But even the temporary discomfort of subjectivity must be treated! And more importantly, the treatment must be enjoyed. Light ethnogastritis contains small doses of evil and therefore the possibility of a vaccine. What could quickly become fear, or hate, is turned into love.

South Korea, 2009

I am hiking up a steep path in the forest of the Seoraksan National Park. A warm breeze, from time to time, dries my sweating temples. Above my head, two raptors fly in high and wide circles. As I reach a rest area a forty-something man, sitting with two women, invites me to their table. They are drinking a bottle of liquor I have never tasted before. He looks delighted to meet a foreigner, and asks me in Korean if I would care for a drink. Not that I understand Korean, but his intention is obvious from the bottle and the empty plastic glass he has lifted up, grinning, from the table. I nod and smile and even clap my hands a few times to show my appreciation. I take a sip; it tastes a bit like Japanese sake. I ask them in English if this is made from rice, but they have no idea what I mean. I say "rice" in Japanese, in case the word left a mark in Korea, but they laugh and reply in Korean. I pick up a twig from the floor and draw grains of rice on the moss-covered table, but realise they do not look real enough and start laughing. They laugh with me, and I feel comfortable already. The man grabs the twig, and draws what I identify as an ear of corn.

"Is it corn? Corn?," I venture.

"Corn?," he repeats.

"Corn ...", one of the women giggles.

I eat in front of them an imaginary ear of corn, gnawing at it from left to right, and again from left to right. They nod excitedly, release a shout of victory and we all laugh heartily. Corn it was. We keep gesticulating for a while and manage to learn a few things about each other. At some point in the conversation the man points at himself and throw punches in the air.

"You're a boxer?," I say.

"No ..."

I point at him and punch an imaginary opponent.

"You like boxing? Fighting?"

"No, no ..." he giggles, shaking his head. Then he adds:

"International," points at himself, and reaches into his pocket for a business card. I bow my head a little as he gives it to me. It is written in Korean on one side and in English on the other. It says on the top: "World Boxing Council—Referee." Below are his name and contact details.

"Ah!," I exclaim before we laugh together again.

They invite me to join them until the waterfall, and the couple of hours I spend with them are most entertaining. We keep talking on the way, I in English and they in Korean. An outside observer (or better, someone watching our hike with subtitles) would probably find it as comical as a scene of Jarmusch's Ghost Dog, in which two friends "converse," one in English, the other in French, without understanding the other's language; and in an ideal situation we would even make sense, like the Korean and Japanese lovers of Kim Ki-duk's Dream. Yet we already exchange so much, pulling faces, shrugging, clapping, miming, and often bursting out laughing. I feel a deep affection towards the international referee I have just met. We smile at each other, read each other's eyes, and come to understand each other. For a couple of hours I feel closer to him than to my closest friends.

The content of this communication was less significant than our emotional involvement in it, than our pleasure of learning from each other, of treating each laborious understanding of some triviality in our little lives as a major discovery. I saw myself in them and they saw themselves in me. Our encounter had assassinated language, and instead we were engaged in a dreamy, surrealist, emotive act of knowledge. Just as dreams are exclusively concerned with the ego and as such the "royal road" to ourselves, the poetic encounter and poetic writing in anthropology articulate subjectivity and alterity in the emotional density of the *relationship*, the between-us, showing a "royal road" to others. As Borges (1966: 184–185) writes in a poem:

> Sometimes in the evenings a face
> Looks at us from the depth of a mirror;
> Art must be like this mirror
> Which reveals our own face.

4
Conclusion

> **Abstract:** *This chapter recapitulates the main argument and points at directions for reintroducing emotions into anthropological writing. Through the parable of the "Wild Boy" that medicine endeavoured, in vain, to civilise, this conclusion restates that science builds on dreams, fantasies, myths, and the frustrations they result in. Furthermore, violent and erotic tensions condition knowledge about others.*
>
> *Anthropology can therefore move away from the guilt that paralyses it. It can gain impetus from the passions that make us human. It can turn guilt and abjection into creative erotic writing. It can escape politically correct legitimisations. It can describe everything, borrowing from the narrative techniques of masterly writing in world literature.*
>
> *It can do all that, and it probably should.*
>
> Bouchetoux, François. *Writing Anthropology: A Call for Uninhibited Methods.* New York: Palgrave Macmillan, 2014.
> DOI: 10.1057/9781137404176.0007.

I was baptised and spent many summer holidays where Victor, the "Wild Boy of Aveyron," was found in 1797. Jean Marc Gaspard Itard was the physician who set out to educate and "civilise" him. After five years however, Victor had not made much progress and Dr. Itard eventually renounced his method, lest it would degrade them both. Victor was not the virtuous and innocent man in a state of nature that Rousseau celebrates, but an animal, and a pretty weak one at that—devoid of emotional intelligence, he led a precarious and aimless life of subsistence (Itard does not consider how strong Victor must have been to survive on his own). Working with Victor, Itard also became increasingly aware of the limitations of science, and in particular of the shaky boundaries between saneness and madness, good and evil (Gineste, 2004).

In the *Analects* (IV. 3), Confucius writes that "only one who is wholly human can truly love and truly despise others." This idea of what it means to be wholly *human* is echoed in an important tradition of thought—the Marquis de Sade's philosophy of good and evil; George Bataille's analyses of excess and dilapidation; Michel Foucault's studies of classification and madness; and cases such as Pierre Rivière (Foucault, 1994c), Victor, or the two "wild" girls found in the region of Midnapore in India (Le Breton, 2001: 14–15), which seem to validate this tradition: "in the most simple types of insanity, the wholly human can be recognised in the madman" (Gineste, 2004: 434).

I would like to point out, in addition, that the relationship between Itard and Victor represents an appealing parable of ethnography. Itard emerges as a disappointed figure, confessing that his hard work did not produce what he expected; at the same time he understands and epitomises the role of illusions, of imaginary scenarios in the making of science. As Gaston Bachelard ceaselessly recalled, knowledge builds on dreams, fantasies, myths, and importantly the frustrations and disappointments of a reality that does not match such "unreasonable" expectations. This story, which after all is that of a long series of instructive failures, corresponds to my own experience and to my reading of cultural anthropology. Current anthropology is still "in the middle of a period of soul-searching about the morality of fieldwork relations and the ethico-political implications of ethnography" (Robben and Sluka, 2007: 23). But perhaps anthropologists could challenge the idea that they moved from one type of methodology (racist, civilisationist) to another (reflexive). Only historical circumstances determined the mode of writing, while the core motivation, that of "knowing" and above all tolerating the Other, was invariant through time. Thus reflexivity, or at least doubts concerning the conditions of knowledge formation, existed in 19th-century travelogues. Pierre Loti's sincere reports are of outstanding literary value, inspiring not guilt, but an awareness that the Other is worth knowing. His texts on Japan combine the racist flavour of colonial times and an interest in the Other that surpasses many contemporary ethnographies.

Too much anthropology feels too guilty to express the curiosity and spontaneous passions of new encounters. Too much anthropology lies to itself, showing itself under the most flattering light, relegating its evils to the sacred or the intimate that cannot be divulged lest it compromises the "love of people" that drives and defines it. There are two main lies, two strategies of evasion: one is to prove that nothing resists anthropology via the myth of the victorious interpreter, who managed to overcome complex situations; the other is to assert that failure is meaningful, when it might not be (most failures only refer to themselves). In practice, some anthropologists will admit they did not really integrate the field; others will say that they were perfectly integrated. And is successful integration with the people you write about vital? Some think that it is, and feel guilty; others raise problems of integration and linger on the epistemological challenges of ethnography. But most of these challenges also involve guilt, as described earlier in the book.

Guilt produces methodological insights but also freezes anthropology, which often finds itself locked in a spiral of self-deception, or what Sartre used to call "bad faith." According to Bruckner (1983, 2010), modern Western thought is pervaded with Judeo-Christian guilt, which emphasises the violence of the West *ad nauseam*. Through such self-loathing, evil acquires the indispensable face of the Euro-American, the face of "white ferocity" (Plumelle-Uribe, 2001) responsible for the slave trade, colonisations, and Nazism. Bruckner (2010: 34, 73, 101) argues, however, that self-denunciation is an indirect form of self-glorification. This "paternalism of the guilty conscience" remains a passion for domination, masochistically turned against oneself the better to take pride in exporting humility and wisdom. Thus Christianity indirectly reassures its believers that they are good, because they know they are evil. Western culture does not "repent" of its sin but remains attached to it; it feeds on remorse. This narcissistic logic of self-flagellation hardly conceals Western insensitivity or disdain for distant customs. Western people lie to themselves about themselves, and more importantly close themselves to others. For Bruckner it is only by becoming friends of themselves that westerners can befriend others again. He calls for a "creative barbarity" that seeks to transform the hideous crimes of the West into generous passions, to celebrate heroes not traitors, and to focus on what is the best in "us" westerners: we ought to recognise the inhumanity within each of us, so as to sublimate it towards positive ends.

I would tend to agree with Bruckner's analysis, but also believe that the simple (and vague) "solution" he promotes might not do much if it does not draft methodological directions. This book has attempted to underline that reading, writing, and thinking were first and foremost methodological activities—that what we call "research" means, for the most part, methodology. In the anthropological context, guilt offers not just opportunities to condemn or celebrate it, but more importantly possibilities for emotional language and uninhibited writing. Le Breton (2001: 92, 98) reminds us, in this respect, that there is an intelligibility of emotion, a logic that emotions pursue, and that even the most rigorous thought is conditioned by affects. Proust's *Search of Lost Time*, which Le Breton frequently cites, communicates the sensations that make existence meaningful and worth narrating. Anthropologists can, and should, use guilt to emancipate their discipline, not to torture it or downgrade it with politically correct legitimisations. It is time to represent hatred as much as love, disintegration as much as integration. Fabian (2000: 281), who argues among others (e.g., Olivier de Sardan, 2005: 54–55; Jolles, 2006: 38) that much of anthropology has not freed itself from the colonialist logic of domination, would even go further in this direction. Why not move away from these questions of guilt (and from self-interestedness parading as "reflexivity") and acknowledge a *present* error, "a kind of failure that reaches beyond individuals in the past"? Why not describe everything, including crude violence that is best understood in its complexities? Why not let the politically incorrect speak? Failure to cope with cruelty, intolerance, racism, are human—why not spell them out, throw them up, represent them in their most atrocious forms? Pierre Loti has bequeathed to us an invaluable exoticism that only a poetry of uninhibited racism could make possible. Anthropologists, write your passions as you experience them. Be a racist, a groupie, a hypocrite. Be, once again, an explorer. Love and hate your natives and yourself, travelling and explorers.

Fire

The "fire" chapter opened with Bachelard's intuition that the emotions and sensations of daydreams spark scientific knowledge like the match starts a fire. Sitting by this cosy fire, feeling its warmth, hearing its crackling, Bachelard invents the story behind the flickers and restless glows, approaching reality via imagination, analytics via poetics. Anthropology can in the same way understand itself by either making up its topics or putting its real topics in conversation with the imaginary. At stake is as much an "imaginary anthropology" as Crapanzano's (2004: 1) "anthropology of the imagination." Fabian (2000: 208) advocates "acts of intellectual empathy and imagination" that require us "to go beyond ourselves" and "approach the ecstatic." An alternative expression that would stress the imaginary potential and duty of anthropology is "*dream* anthropology," which combines the poetics of disturbing dreams, of forbidden passions, to anthropological ideals. Such anthropology is essentially emotional (Wolcott, 2005: 59).

Water

The "water" chapter described emotional complications of engaging with others—"ethnogastritis." Bronislaw Malinowski (1922: vi), according to James Frazer's preface of his most famous opus, "is constantly at pains to discover the emotional as well as the rational basis of human action." My account of ethnogastritis had two simple objectives. One was to highlight the communicative potential of non-discursive knowledge in anthropology; the other was to develop writing strategies on the basis of this potential. The point of such anthropology is no longer to show empathy or understand the "point of view" of a community, but to throw oneself into this community; to let oneself collapse into its excesses and absurdities, like actors and spectators in the plays of Samuel Beckett and Eugène Ionesco; to experience life without fishing for meanings in everything and everyone; to report nothing but emotions; to write nothing but poetry. The postmodern movement rightly insisted that anthropology become a branch of poetry, that is, as Michael Taussig (2010: xi) has it, "a matter of finding the words and rhythm of language that resonate with what we are writing about. To put it crudely: anthropology studies culture, but in the process 'makes' culture as well." As a result and perhaps ironically, current anthropology attempts to regain the literary dimension that old travelogues used to display (Fabian, 2000: 249). These anthropological poetics, however, should not exclude the recording of commonsense—the more dispassionate, list-like, and nearly aimless descriptions that make Georges Perec's novels "ethnographic" according to Howard Becker (2001). While anthropology should encourage experiments with writing, it does not have to be reduced to them. Innovations are not just stylistic; they are also conceptual—they concern "the use and organisation of evidence" (Borneman and Hammoudi, 2009: 18). I believe there is much poetry in the ordinary anyway. All we need to do is look *harder*, start *afresh*, write *again*.

All anthropologists face the same question: how to describe? Positivists seek objectivity, constructionists are more comfortable with subjectivity, but essentially they write with the same aim of being truer and closer to reality. So this question reiterates what researchers should constantly ask themselves, because it shapes their conclusions, because "everything" is, in a way, methodological. There are intimate or spectacular things in fiction (in literature, in cinema) that anthropologists are just not willing or not allowed to describe. I think it is worth wondering where these restrictions come from, and what could be deployed without them. Anthropology could borrow a little more from the narrative techniques of great literature, for example. Good love stories say important things about human relations. And even if the same cultures are studied over and over again, writers manage to produce different and original claims because of the way in which they tell the story.

Finally, why should anthropology target knowledge since it constantly stresses that its meaning shifts across cultures? To write the present is to be always already untrue—people have moved, people have changed, people have died, including the anthropologist. Perhaps anthropology should accept that its very significance does not belong to the present, and that it will not be always significant. The idea of ethnogastritis tells us that good ethnography involves continuous presence and rapport (not everyone will know how to build it), as well as forcing oneself to see-touch-smell-hear-taste everything, and do everything (including what one does not want to do). While vision is an "active sense" and traditional source of knowledge, all other "passive" senses make us *vulnerable* (Fabian, 2000: 185); it is precisely on this vulnerability that Behar (1996) advises us to build. Good ethnography involves a risk of transgressing rules or even suffering eviction from the community. Fabian (2000: 280) shows that the various ways in which we can lose control and be "out of our minds," following fits of desperation and violence, erotic tensions, and the like, is a condition of knowledge about others.

Ethnogastritis is a state of mind and a method. It is repugnance at living with others and at the same time a fecund virus, which blows away the airs of seriousness and necessity anthropology often adorns itself with. As long as the toxicity of fieldwork methods is actively grasped, then it can become the poison that contains its own cure; then it can be sublimated through the sensual writing of poignant memories. Ethnogastritis, exuberant management of excess, elevates anthropology to the art of being with others rather than the study of others. Anthropology takes a giant leap, in this way, from the boredom of dry observations to the effervescence of life. By way of illustration, this leap compares to that between the biological or medical knowledge of copulation, as cold and dead as raw meat, and the non-knowledge of eroticism, inner experience of spasmodic sensations that colour from deep inside our imagination—as warm and wet and alive as our pounding organs.

References

Agar, Michael H. (1980) *The Professional Stranger: An Informal Introduction to Ethnography*, New York: Academic Press.

Agar, Michael H. (1995) "Literary Journalism as Ethnography: Exploring the Excluded Middle," in Van Maanen, John (ed.), *Representation in Ethnography*, Thousand Oaks: Sage, 112–129.

Alsup, Janet (2004) "Protean Subjectivities: Qualitative Research and the Inclusion of the Personal," in Brown, Stephen Gilbert, and Sidney I. Dobrin (eds.), *Ethnography Unbound: From Theory Shock to Critical Praxis*, New York: State University of New York Press, 219–237.

Altork, Kate (1995) "Walking the Fire Line: The Erotic Dimension of the Fieldwork Experience," in Kulick, Don, and Margaret Willson (eds.), *Taboo: Sex, Identity, and Erotic Subjectivity in Anthropological Fieldwork*, London: Routledge, 107–139.

Amirou, Rachid (2012) *L'Imaginaire Touristique*, Paris: CNRS éditions.

Amit, Vered (2000) "Introduction: Constructing the Field," in Amit, Vered (ed.), *Constructing the Field: Ethnographic Fieldwork in the Contemporary World*, London and New York: Routledge, 1–18.

Anderson, Elijah (2006) "Jelly's Place: An Ethnographic Memoir," in Hobbs, Dick, and Richard Wright (eds.), *The SAGE Handbook of Fieldwork*, London, Thousand Oaks, and New Delhi: Sage, 39–58.

References

Appadurai, Arjun (1996) *Modernity at Large: Cultural Dimensions of Globalization*, Minneapolis: The University of Minnesota Press.
Armstrong, Gary (1993) "Like that Desmond Morris?" in Hobbs, D., and T. May (eds.), *Interpreting the Field: Accounts of Ethnography*, Oxford and New York: Clarendon Press, 7–24.
Asad, Talal (1973) *Reinventing Anthropology*, New York: Vintage.
Atkinson, Paul (1992) *Understanding Ethnographic Texts*, Newbury Park: Sage.
Aunger, Robert (2004) *Reflexive Ethnographic Science*, Walnut Creek: AltaMira Press.
Bachelard, Gaston (1973) *La Psychanalyse du Feu*, Paris: Gallimard. Original Edition, 1938.
Bachelard, Gaston (1957) *La Poétique de l'Espace*, Paris: Presses Universitaires de France.
Bamford, Sandra Carol, and Joel Robbins (1997) *Fieldwork Revisited: Changing Contexts of Ethnographic Practice in the Era of Globalization*, Arlington: American Anthropological Association.
Barthes, Roland (1970) *L'Empire des Signes*, Paris: Albert Skira.
Bataille, Georges (1957) *L'Érotisme*, Paris: Éditions de Minuit.
Bataille, Georges (1970) *Œuvres Complètes. Vol. 1: Premiers Écrits, 1922–1940*, Paris: Gallimard.
Bataille, Georges (1973a) *Œuvres Complètes. Vol. 2: Écrits Posthumes, 1922–1940*, Paris: Gallimard.
Bataille, Georges (1973b) *Œuvres Complètes. Vol. 5: La Somme Athéologique I*, Paris: Gallimard.
Bataille, Georges (1976) *Œuvres Complètes. Vol. 7*, Paris: Gallimard.
Baudrillard, Jean (1979) *De la Séduction*, Paris: Galilée.
Baudrillard, Jean (1981) *Simulacres et Simulation*, Paris: Galilée.
Becker, Howard (2001) "George Perec's Experiments in Social Description," *Ethnography*, 2 (1): 63–76.
Behar, Ruth (1996) *The Vulnerable Observer: Anthropology That Breaks Your Heart*, Boston: Beacon Press.
Ben-Ari, Eyal (1995) "On Acknowledgements in Ethnographies," in Van Maanen, John (ed.), *Representation in Ethnography*, Thousand Oaks: Sage, 130–164.
Benedict, Ruth (2005) *The Crysanthemum and the Sword: Patterns of Japanese Culture*, New York: Mariner Books. Original Edition, 1946.
Benjamin, Walter (1999) *Illuminations*, London: Pimlico.

Berreman, Gerald D. (ed.) (1972) *Hindus of the Himalayas: Ethnography and Change*, Berkeley: University of California Press. Original Edition, 1963.
Bettelheim, Bruno (1976) *The Uses of Enchantment: The Meaning and Importance of Fairy Tales*, New York: Random House.
Bhabha, Homi K. (1989) "Location, Intervention, Incommensurability: A Conversation with Homi Bhabha," *Emergences*, 1 (1): 63–88.
Biehl, João, and Peter Locke (2010) "Deleuze and the Anthropology of Becoming," *Current Anthropology*, 51 (3): 317–351.
Biehl, João, Good, Byron J., and Arthur Kleinman (eds.) (2007) *Subjectivity: Ethnographic Investigations*, Berkeley and Los Angeles: University of California Press.
Birckhead, Jim (2004) "And I Can't Feel at Home in this World Anymore: Fieldwork in Two Settings," in Hume, Lynne, and Jane Mulcock (eds.), *Anthropologists in the Field: Cases in Participant Observation*, New York: Columbia University Press, 95–107.
Blackwood, Evelyn (1995) "Falling in Love with an-Other Lesbian: Reflections on Identity in Fieldwork," in Kulick, Don, and Margaret Willson (eds.), *Taboo: Sex, Identity and Erotic Subjectivity in Anthropological Fieldwork*, London and New York: Routledge, 51–75.
Boltanski, Luc (2007) *La Souffrance à Distance*, Paris: Gallimard. Original Edition, 1993.
Boorstin, Daniel J. (2012) *The Image: A Guide to Pseudo-Events in America*, New York: Random House. Original Edition, 1961.
Borges, Jorge Luis (1966) *Antología Personal*, Buenos Aires: Sur.
Borneman, John, and Abdellah Hammoudi (eds.) (2009) *Being There: The Fieldwork Encounter and the Making of Truth*, Berkeley and Los Angeles: University of California Press.
Bourdieu, Pierre (1993) *La Misère du Monde*, Paris: Seuil.
Bourgois, Philippe (1991) "Confronting the Ethics of Ethnography: Lessons from Fieldwork in Central America," in Harrison, Faye V. (ed.), *Decolonizing Anthropology: Moving Further Toward an Anthropology for Liberation*, Washington DC: American Anthropological Association, 110–126.
Bowen, Elenore Smith (1954) *Return to Laughter: An Anthropological Novel*, London: Gollancz.
Bowker, Geoffrey C., and Susan Leigh Star (2000) *Sorting Things Out: Classification and Its Consequences*, Cambridge, Mass., and London: MIT Press.

Breton, André (1933) "Le Message Automatique," *Minotaure* 3–4: 55–65.
Brewer, John D. (2000) *Ethnography*, Buckingham: Open University Press.
Briggs, Jean L. (1970) *Never in Anger: Portrait of an Eskimo Family*, Cambridge, Mass.: Harvard University Press.
Brown, Richard H. (1977) *A Poetic for Sociology: Toward a Logic of Discovery for the Human Sciences*, Cambridge, Mass.: Cambridge University Press.
Brown, Stephen Gilbert, and Sidney I. Dobrin (2004) "New Writers of the Cultural Sage: From Postmodern Theory Shock to Critical Praxis," in Brown, Stephen Gilbert, and Sidney I. Dobrin (eds.), *Ethnography Unbound: From Theory Shock to Critical Praxis*, New York: State University of New York Press, 1–12.
Bruckner, Pascal (2010) *The Tyranny of Guilt: An Essay on Western Masochism*, Princeton and Oxford: Princeton University Press.
Bruckner, Pascal (1983) *Le Sanglot de l'Homme Blanc: Tiers-Monde, Culpabilité, Haine de Soi*, Paris: Seuil.
Bruckner, Pascal, and Alain Finkielkraut (1979) *Au Coin de la Rue, l'Aventure*, Paris: Seuil.
Burgess, Robert G. (1982) *Field Research: A Sourcebook and Field Manual*, London and Boston: G. Allen & Unwin.
Caillois, Roger (1993) *L'Homme et le Sacré*, Paris: Gallimard. Original Edition, 1950.
Caputo, Virginia (2000) "At 'Home' and 'Away': Reconfiguring the Field for Late Twentieth-Century Anthropology," in Amit, Vered (ed.), *Constructing the Field: Ethnographic Fieldwork in the Contemporary World*, London and New York: Routledge, 19–31.
Cauvin-Verner, Corinne (2007) *Au Désert: Une Anthropologie du Tourisme dans le Sud Marocain*, Paris: L'Harmattan.
Céline, Louis-Ferdinand (1981) *Romans: Tome 1*, Bibliothèque de la pléiade. Paris: Gallimard.
Certeau, Michel de (1990) *L'Invention du Quotidien, Tome 1: Arts de Faire*, Paris: Gallimard. Original Edition, 1980.
Chagnon, Napoleon A. (1974) *Studying the Yąnomamö*, New York: Holt, Rinehart and Winston, Inc.
Chang, Heewon (2008) *Autoethnography as Method*, Walnut Creek: Left Coast Press, Inc.
Ciccone, Albert, and Alain Ferrant (2009) *Honte, Culpabilité et Traumatisme*, Paris: Dunod.

Clapier-Valladon, Simone (1991) "L'Homme et le Rire," in Jean Poirier (ed.), *Histoire des Mœurs II, Vol. 1: Modes et Modèles*, Paris: Gallimard, 247–297.
Clifford, James (1988) *The Predicament of Culture: Twentieth-Century Ethnography, Literature, and Art*, Cambridge, Mass.: Harvard University Press.
Clifford, James, and George E. Marcus (eds.) (1986) *Writing Culture: The Poetics and Politics of Ethnography*, Berkeley: University of California Press.
Coffey, Amanda (1999) *The Ethnographic Self: Fieldwork and the Representation of Identity*, London, Thousand Oaks and New Delhi: Sage.
Cohen, Anthony P. (1992) "Self-Conscious Anthropology," in Okely, Judith, and Helen Callaway (eds.), *Anthropology and Autobiography*, London and New York: Routledge, 219–238.
Colic-Peisker, Val (2004) "Doing Ethnography in 'One's Own Ethnic Community': The Experience of an Awkward Insider," in Hume, Lynne, and Jane Mulcock (eds.), *Anthropologists in the Field: Cases in Participant Observation*, New York: Columbia University Press, 82–94.
Comaroff, John L., and Jean Comaroff (1992) *Ethnography and the Historical Imagination*, Boulder: Westview Press.
Condominas, Georges (2006) *L'Exotique est Quotidien*, Paris: Pocket. Original Edition, 1965.
Cosgrove, Denis (2008) *Geography & Vision: Seeing, Imagining and Representing the World*, London and New York: I. B. Tauris & Co. Ltd.
Crapanzano, Vincent (1972) *The Fifth World of Forster Bennett: Portrait of a Navajo*, New York: Viking Press.
Crapanzano, Vincent (1980) *Tuhami: Portrait of a Moroccan*, Chicago and London: The University of Chicago Press.
Crapanzano, Vincent (2004) *Imaginative Horizons: An Essay in Literary-Philosophical Anthropology*, Chicago: The University of Chicago Press.
Creighton, Millie (2007) "Dancing Lessons from God: To be the Good Ethnographer or the Good Bad Ethnographer," in Goulet, Jean-Guy A., and Bruce G. Miller (eds.), *Extraordinary Anthropology: Transformations in the Field*, Lincoln and London: The University of Nebraska Press, 380–418.
Crick, Malcom (1992) "Ali and Me: An Essay in Street-Corner Anthropology," in Okely, Judith, and Helen Callaway (eds.),

Anthropology and Autobiography, London and New York: Routledge, 173–189.

Crick, Malcom (1989) "Shifting Identities in the Research Process: An Essay in Personal Anthropology," in Perry, John (ed.), *Doing Fieldwork: Eight Personal Accounts of Social Research*, Sydney: Deakin University Press, 24–40.

Davidson, Joyce, Bondi, Liz, and Mick Smith (eds.) (2007) *Emotional Geographies*, Aldershot: Ashgate Publishing Ltd.

David-Néel, Alexandra (2008) *Voyage d'une Parisienne à Lhassa*, Paris: Pocket. Original Edition, 1927.

Deloria, Vine, Jr. (1973) "Custer Died for Your Sins," in Weaver, Thomas (ed.), *To See Ourselves: Anthropology and Modern Social Issues*, Glenview: Scott, Foresman & Co., pp. 130–137. Original Edition, 1969.

Denzin, Norman K. (1997) *Interpretive Ethnography: Ethnographic Practices for the 21st Century*, Thousand Oaks: Sage.

Denzin, Norman K., and Yvonna S. Lincoln (eds.) (2003) *The Landscape of Qualitative Research: Theories and Issues*, Thousand Oaks: Sage.

Ditton, Jason (1977) *Part-Time Crime: An Ethnography of Fiddling and Pilferage*, London: Macmillan.

Dostoevsky, Fyodor (1992) *The Brothers Karamazov*, New York: Everyman's Library. Original Edition, 1880.

Dubisch, Jill (1995) "Lovers in the Field: Sex, Dominance, and the Female Anthropologist," in Kulick, Don, and Margaret Willson (eds.), *Taboo: Sex, Identity and Erotic Subjectivity in Anthropological Fieldwork*, London and New York: Routledge, 29–50.

Dumont, Jean-Paul (1991) *The Headman and I: Ambiguity and Ambivalence in the Fieldworking Experience*, Long Grove: Waveland Press Inc. Original Edition, 1978.

Dwyer, Kevin (1977) "On the Dialogic of Fieldwork," *Dialectical Anthropology* 2: 143–51.

Dyck, Noel (2000) "Home Field Advantage? Exploring the Social Construction of Children's Sports," in Amit, Vered (ed.), *Constructing the Field: Ethnographic Fieldwork in the Contemporary World*, London and New York: Routledge, 32–53.

Eco, Umberto (1995) *Travels in Hyperreality*, Boston: First Harvest. Original Edition, 1986.

Eliade, Mircea (1989a) *Histoire des Croyances et des Idées Religieuses /1: De l'Âge de la Pierre aux Mystères d'Eleusis*, Paris: Bibliothèque Historique Payot.

Eliade, Mircea (1989b) *Histoire des Croyances et des Idées Religieuses /2: De Gautama Bouddha au Triomphe du Christianisme*, Paris: Bibliothèque Historique Payot.
Eliade, Mircea (1992) *Le Chamanisme et les Techniques Archaïques de l'Extase*, Paris: Bibliothèque Historique Payot.
Elias, Norbert (2000) *The Civilizing Process: Sociogenetic and Psychogenetic Investigations*, Malden: Blackwell. Original Edition, 1939.
Ellis, Carolyn (2003) *The Ethnographic I: A Methodological Novel about Autoethnography*, Walnut Creek: AltaMira Press.
Ellis, Carolyn (2008) *Revision: Autoethnographic Reflections on Life and Work*, Walnut Creek: Left Coast Press, Inc.
Etherington, Kim (2004) *Becoming a Reflexive Researcher: Using Our Selves in Research*, London: Jessica Kingsley Publishers.
Evans-Pritchard, Edward E. (1940) *The Nuer: A Description of the Modes of Livelihood and Political Institutions of a Nilotic People*, Oxford: Oxford University Press.
Fabian, Johannes (1983) *Time and the Other: How Anthropology Makes Its Object*, New York: Columbia University Press.
Fabian, Johannes (2000) *Out of Our Minds: Reason and Madness in the Exploration of Central Africa*, Berkeley, Los Angeles, and London: University of California Press.
Favret-Saada, Jeanne (1980) *Deadly Words: Witchcraft in the Bocage*, Cambridge, Mass.: Cambridge University Press.
Fetterman, David M. (1989) *Ethnography: Step by Step*, Newbury Park: Sage.
Firth, Raymond (2004) *We, the Tikopia*, London: Routledge. Original Edition, 1936.
Fischer, Michael M. J., and Mehdi Abedi (1990) *Debating Muslims: Cultural Dialogues in Postmodernity and Tradition*, Madison: University of Wisconsin Press.
Flaubert, Gustave (2001) *Madame Bovary*, Paris: Flammarion. Original Edition, 1857.
Forsey, Martin (2004) "'He's not a Spy; He's One of Us': Ethnographic Positioning in a Middle-Class Setting," in Hume, Lynne, and Jane Mulcock (eds.), *Anthropologists in the Field: Cases in Participant Observation*, New York: Columbia University Press, 59–70.
Forster, John (1964) "The Sociological Consequences of Tourism," *International Journal of Comparative Sociology*, 5 (2): 217–227.

Foucault, Michel (1994a) "Des Espaces Autres," *Dits et Écrits: 1954–1988*, Vol. IV: 1980–1988, Paris: Gallimard, 752–762. Original Edition, 1967.
Foucault, Michel (1994b) *Histoire de la Sexualité I: La Volonté de Savoir*, Paris: Gallimard. Original Edition, 1976.
Foucault, Michel (1994c) *Moi, Pierre Rivière, Ayant Égorgé ma Mère, ma Soeur et mon Frère...: Un cas de Parricide au XIXe siècle*, Paris: Folio Histoire. Original Edition, 1973.
Foucault, Michel (2004) *Utopies et Hétérotopies* [audio CD], Ina, Mémoire Vive.
Fox, Karen V. (1996) "Silent Voices: A Subversive Reading of Child Abuse," in Ellis, Carolyn, and Arthur P. Bochner (eds.), *Composing Ethnography*, Walnut Creek: AltaMira, 330–356.
Freud, Sigmund (1998) *Totem and Taboo*, New York: Dover Thrift Editions. Original Edition, 1918.
Freud, Sigmund (1962) *Three Essays on the Theory of Sexuality*, London: Hogarth Press. Original Edition, 1905.
Freud, Sigmund (1991) *The Interpretation of Dreams*, London: Penguin Books. Original Edition, 1900.
Gardner, Peter M. (2007) "On Puzzling Wavelengths," in Goulet, Jean-Guy A., and Bruce G. Miller (eds.), *Extraordinary Anthropology: Transformations in the Field*, Lincoln and London: The University of Nebraska Press, 17–35.
Gearing, Jean (1995) "Fear and Loving in the West Indies: Research from the Heart (As Well As the Head)," in Kulick, Don, and Margaret Willson (eds.), *Taboo: Sex, Identity and Erotic Subjectivity in Anthropological Fieldwork*, London and New York: Routledge, 186–218.
Geertz, Clifford (1973) *The Interpretation of Cultures: Selected Essays*, New York: Basic Books.
Geertz, Clifford (1988) *Works and Lives: The Anthropologist as Author*, Stanford: Stanford University Press.
Geertz, Clifford (2000) *Local Knowledge: Further Essays in Interpretive Anthropology*, New York: Basic Books.
Geertz, Clifford (2012) *Life Among the Anthros and Other Essays*, Princeton and Oxford: Princeton University Press.
Gessel, Van C., and Tomone Matsumoto (eds.) (1985) *The Shōwa Anthology: Modern Japanese Short Stories*, Tokyo: Kodansha International.
Giard, Agnès (2007) *L'Imaginaire Érotique au Japon*, Paris: Albin Michel.

Gineste, Thierry (2004) *Victor de l'Aveyron: Dernier Enfant Sauvage, Premier Enfant Fou*, Paris: Hachette/Pluriel.
Goffman, Ervin (1959) *The Presentation of Self in Everyday Life*, New York: Anchor Books.
Goody, Jack (2010) *Myth, Ritual and the Oral*, Cambridge, Mass.: Cambridge University Press.
Gorzelsky, Gwen (2004) "Shifting Figures: Rhetorical Ethnography," in Brown, Stephen Gilbert, and Sidney I. Dobrin (eds.), *Ethnography Unbound: From Theory Shock to Critical Praxis*, New York: State University of New York Press, 73–98.
Goulet, Jean-Guy A., and Bruce G. Miller (eds.) (2007) *Extraordinary Anthropology: Transformations in the Field*, Lincoln and London: The University of Nebraska Press.
Graburn, Nelson H. H. (1983) "The Anthropology of Tourism," *Annals of Tourism Research*, 10 (1): 9–33.
Gregory, Derek (1994) *Geographical Imaginations*, Cambridge, Mass.: Blackwell.
Grey, Chris (2009) *A Very Short, Fairly Interesting and Reasonably Cheap Book about Studying Organizations*, London: Sage.
Grignon, Claude, and Jean-Claude Passeron (1989) *Le Savant et le Populaire: Misérabilisme et Populisme en Sociologie et en Littérature*, Paris: Seuil.
Gupta, Akhil, and James Ferguson (1992) "Beyond 'Culture': Space, Identity, and the Politics of Difference," *Cultural Anthropology*, 7 (1): 6–23.
Hagège, Claude (2012) *Contre la Pensée Unique*, Paris: Odile Jacob.
Hammersley, Martyn, and Paul Atkinson (eds.) (1995) *Ethnography: Principles in Practice*, London and New York: Routledge.
Hammersley, Martyn, and Paul Atkinson (eds.) (2007) *Ethnography: Principles in Practice*, London and New York: Routledge.
Hand, Séan (2004) *Michel Leiris: Writing the Self*, Cambridge, Mass.: Cambridge University Press.
Hanson, Susan S. (2004) "Critical Auto/Ethnography: A Constructive Approach to Research in the Composition Classroom," in Brown, Stephen Gilbert, and Sidney I. Dobrin (eds.), *Ethnography Unbound: From Theory Shock to Critical Praxis*, New York: State University of New York Press, 183–200.
Harvey, Graham (2004) "Performing and Constructing Research as Guesthood in the Study of Religions," in Hume, Lynne, and Jane

Mulcock (eds.), *Anthropologists in the Field: Cases in Participant Observation*, New York: Columbia University Press, 168–182.

Hastrup, Kirsten (1992) "Writing Ethnography: State of the Art," in Okely, Judith, and Helen Callaway (eds.), *Anthropology and Autobiography*, London and New York: Routledge, 115–131.

Hastrup, Kirsten, and Karen Fog Olwig (1997) "Introduction," in Olwig, Karen Fog, and Kirsten Hastrup (eds.), *Siting Culture: The Shifting Anthropological Object*, London and New York: Routledge, 1–14.

Hearn, Lafcadio (2007) *Glimpses of Unfamiliar Japan, Vol. 2*, New York: Cosimo. Original Edition, 1894.

Hendry, Joy (1992) "The Paradox of Friendship in the Field: Analysis of a Long Term Anglo-Japanese Relationship," in Okely, Judith, and Helen Callaway (eds.), *Anthropology and Autobiography*, London and New York: Routledge, 161–171.

Hergé (1993) *Tintin au Congo*, Tournai: Casterman. Original black and white edition, 1931.

Herzfeld, Michael (2001) *Anthropology: Theoretical Practice in Culture and Society*, Malden: Blackwell.

Herzfeld, Michael (1997) *Cultural Intimacy: Social Poetics in the Nation-State*, New York: Routledge.

Hine, Christine (2001) "Ethnography in the Laboratory," in Gellner, David N., and Eric Hirsch (eds.), *Inside Organizations: Anthropologists at Work*, Oxford and New York: Berg, 61–76.

Horner, Bruce (2004) "Critical Ethnography, Ethics, and Work: Rearticulating Labour," in Brown, Stephen Gilbert, and Sidney I. Dobrin (eds.), *Ethnography Unbound: From Theory Shock to Critical Praxis*, New York: State University of New York Press, 13–34.

Hours, Bernard, and Monique Selim (2010) *Anthropologie Politique de la Globalisation,* Paris: L'Harmattan.

Huizer, Gerrit, and Bruce Mannheim (eds.) (1979) *The Politics of Anthropology: From Colonialism and Sexism Toward a View from Below*, The Hague: Mouton Publishers.

Hume, Lynne, and Jane Mulcock (2004) "Introduction: Awkward Spaces, Productive Places," in Hume, Lynne, and Jane Mulcock (eds.), *Anthropologists in the Field: Cases in Participant Observation*, New York: Columbia University Press, xi–xxvii.

Hymes, Dell H. (ed.) (1999) *Reinventing Anthropology*, Ann Arbor: The University of Michigan Press. Original Edition, 1972.

Inda, Jonathan X., and Renato Rosaldo (eds.) (2002) *The Anthropology of Globalization: A Reader*, Malden and Oxford: Blackwell.
Jackson, Jean E. (1995) ""Déjà Entendu": The Liminal Qualities of Anthropological Fieldnotes," in Van Maanen, John (ed.), *Representation in Ethnography*, Thousand Oaks: Sage, 36–78.
Jackson, Anthony (ed.) (1987) *Anthropology at Home*, London: Tavistock.
Jackson, Michael (ed.) (1996) *Things as They Are: New Directions in Phenomenological Anthropology*.
Jackson, Michael (2005) *Existential Anthropology: Events, Exigencies and Effects*, New York and Oxford: Berghahn Books.
Jameson, Fredric (1983) *The Political Unconscious: Narrative as a Socially Symbolic Act*, London: Methuen.
Jay, Martin (1993) *Downcast Eyes: The Denigration of Vision in Twentieth-Century French Thought*, Berkeley: University of California Press.
Jolles, Carol Zane (2006) "Listening to Elders, Working with the Youth," in Stern, Pamela, and Lisa Stevenson (eds.), *Critical Inuit Studies: An Anthology of Contemporary Arctic Ethnography*, Lincoln and London: University of Nebraska Press, 35–53.
Jorgensen, Danny L. (1989) *Participant Observation: A Methodology for Human Studies*, Newbury Park: Sage.
Josephides, Lisette (1997) "Representing the Anthropologist's Predicament," in James, Alison, Hockey, Jennifer L., and Andrew H. Dawson (eds.), *After Writing Culture: Epistemology and Praxis in Contemporary Anthropology*, London and New York: Routledge, 16–33.
Kafka, Franz (2000) *The Trial*, London: Penguin Classics. Original Edition, 1925.
Kelly, Patty (2004) "Awkward Intimacies: Prostitution, Politics, and Fieldwork in Urban Mexico," in Hume, Lynne, and Jane Mulcock (eds.), *Anthropologists in the Field: Cases in Participant Observation*, New York: Columbia University Press, 3–17.
Kenna, Margaret E. (1992) "Changing Places and Altered Perspectives: Research on a Greek Island in the 1960s and in the 1980s," in Okely, Judith, and Helen Callaway (eds.), *Anthropology and Autobiography*, London and New York: Routledge, 145–160.
Kenny, Paul (1995) *Dés Pipés à Taipei pour Coplan*, Paris: Fleuve Noir.
Kerr, Alex (1996) *Lost Japan*, Hawthorn: Lonely Planet Publications.
Killick, Andrew P. (1995) "The Penetrating Intellect: On Being White, Straight, and Male in Korea," in Kulick, Don, and Margaret Willson

(eds.), *Taboo: Sex, Identity and Erotic Subjectivity in Anthropological Fieldwork*, London and New York: Routledge, 76–106.

Kim, Choong Soon (2002) *One Anthropologist, Two Worlds: Three Decades of Reflexive Fieldwork in North America and Asia*, Knoxville: The University of Tennessee Press.

Klein, Melanie (1975) "On Observing the Behaviour of Young Infants (1952)," *Envy and Gratitude and Other Works 1946–1963*, New York: The Free Press, 94–121.

Knowles, Caroline (2000) "Here and There: Doing Transnational Fieldwork," in Amit, Vered (ed.), *Constructing the Field: Ethnographic Fieldwork in the Contemporary World*, London and New York: Routledge, 54–70.

Kral, Michael J., and Lori Idlout (2006) "Participatory Anthropology in Nunavut," in Stern, Pamela, and Lisa Stevenson (eds.), *Critical Inuit Studies: An Anthology of Contemporary Arctic Ethnography*, Lincoln and London: University of Nebraska Press, 54–70.

Kristeva, Julia (1980) *Pouvoirs de l'Horreur: Essai sur l'Abjection*, Paris: Seuil.

Kulick, Don, and Margaret Willson (eds.) (1995) *Taboo: Sex, Identity and Erotic Subjectivity in Anthropological Fieldwork*, London and New York: Routledge.

Lacan, Jacques (2004) *Le Séminaire, Livre X: L'Angoisse. 1962–1963*, Paris: Seuil.

Lacan, Jacques (1977) *Écrits: A Selection*, London: Tavistock/Routledge.

Lacoste-Dujardin, Camille (1977) *Dialogue de Femmes en Ethnologie*, Paris: François Maspero.

Lassiter, Luke Eric (2001) "From 'Reading Over the Shoulders of Natives' to 'Reading Alongside Natives', Literally: Toward a Collaborative and Reciprocal Ethnography," *Journal of Anthropological Research*, 57 (2): 137–149.

Lassiter, Luke Eric (2005) "Collaborative Ethnography and Public Anthropology," *Current Anthropology*, 46 (1): 83–106.

Le Breton, David (2001) *Les Passions Ordinaires: Anthropologie des Émotions*, Paris: Armand Colin. Original Edition, 1998.

Lee, Molly (2006) "Flora and Me," in Stern, Pamela, and Lisa Stevenson (eds.), *Critical Inuit Studies: An Anthology of Contemporary Arctic Ethnography*, Lincoln and London: University of Nebraska Press, 25–34.

Lefebvre, Henri (2000) *La Production de l'Espace*, 4ᵉ édition, Paris: Anthropos. Original Edition, 1974.
Leiris, Michel (1988) *L'Afrique Fantôme*, Paris: Gallimard. Original Edition, 1934.
Leiris, Michel (1976) *La Règle du Jeu. I. Biffures*, Paris: Gallimard. Original Edition, 1948.
Leiris, Michel (1973) *L'Âge d'Homme*, Paris: Gallimard. Original Edition, 1939.
Lévi-Strauss, Claude (1955) *Tristes Tropiques*, Paris: Plon.
Lien, Marianne E. (1997) *Marketing and Modernity*, Oxford and New York: Berg.
Lippit, Seiji M. (2001) "I-Novel," in Buckley, Sandra (ed.), *Encyclopedia of Contemporary Japanese Culture*, London and New York: Routledge, 204–205.
Loti, Pierre (1925a) *Madame Chrysanthème*, Paris: Calmann-Lévy. Original Edition, 1887.
Loti, Pierre (1925b) *Japoneries d'Automne*, Paris: Calmann-Lévy. Original Edition, 1889.
Lyotard, Jean-François (1979) *La Condition Postmoderne*, Paris: Éditions de Minuit.
MacCannell, Dean (1999) *The Tourist: A New Theory of the Leisure Class*, Berkeley: University of California Press.
MacCannell, Dean (1992) *Empty Meeting Grounds: The Tourist Papers*, London and New York: Routledge.
Madison, D. Soyini (2011) *Critical Ethnography: Methods, Ethics and Performance*, London and New York: Sage.
Maget, Marcel (1968) "Ethnographie Européenne," in Poirier, Jean (ed.), *Ethnologie Générale*, Paris: Gallimard, Bibliothèque de la Pléiade, 1247–1338.
Malinowski, Bronislaw (2002) *Argonauts of the Western Pacific: An Account of Native Enterprise and Adventure in the Archipelagoes of Melanesian New Guinea*, London: Routledge. Original Edition, 1922.
Malinowski, Bronislaw (1989) *A Diary in the Strict Sense of the Term*, Stanford: Stanford University Press. Original Edition, 1967.
Marcus, George E. (ed.) (1992) *Rereading Cultural Anthropology*, Durham: Duke University Press.
Marcus, George E. (1998) *Ethnography Through Thick and Thin*, Princeton: Princeton University Press.

Marcus, George E. (1995) "Ethnography In/Of the World System: The Emergence of Multi-Sited Ethnography," *Annual Review of Anthropology*, 24: 95–117.

Marcus, George E., and Michael M. J. Fischer (1986) *Anthropology as Cultural Critique: An Experimental Moment in the Human Sciences*, Chicago: University of Chicago Press.

Markowitz, Fran, and Michael Ashkenazi (eds.) (1999) *Sex, Sexuality, and the Anthropologist*, Chicago: The University of Illinois Press.

Martin, Christian (1996) "De l'ethnologie à l'ethnographie: *L'Empire des signes* de Roland Barthes," in Norman, Buford (ed.), *Ethnography in French Literature*, French Literature Series Vol. XXIII, Amsterdam: Rodopi, 13–26.

Mauss, Marcel (1926) *Manuel d'Ethnographie*, Paris: Gallimard.

McKenzie Stevens, Sharon (2004) "Debating Ecology: Ethnographic Writing that "Makes a Difference," in Brown, Stephen Gilbert, and Sidney I. Dobrin (eds.), *Ethnography Unbound: From Theory Shock to Critical Praxis*, New York: State University of New York Press, 157–180.

Meneley, Anne, and Donna Young (2005) (eds.) *Auto-Ethnographies: The Anthropology of Academic Practices*, Toronto: The University of Toronto Press.

Merleau-Ponty, Maurice (1945) *Phénoménologie de la Perception*, Paris: Gallimard.

Michaux, Henri (1968) *Ecuador: Journal de Voyage*, Paris: Gallimard. Original Edition, 1929.

Michaux, Henri (1967) *Un Barbare en Asie*, Paris: Gallimard. Original Edition, 1933.

Michel, Franck (2004) *Désirs d'Ailleurs: Essai d'Anthropologie des Voyages*, Quebec City: Presses de l'Université de Laval. Original Edition, 2000.

Miller, Daniel (1997) *Capitalism: An Ethnographic Approach*, Oxford and Washington: Berg.

Moeran, Brian (1996) *A Japanese Advertising Agency: An Anthropology of Media and Markets*, Honolulu: University of Hawaii Press.

Moore, Alexander (1980) "Walt Disney World: Bounded Ritual Space and the Playful Pilgrimage Center," *Anthropological Quarterly*, 53(4): 207–218.

Morton, Helen (1995) "My 'Chastity Belt': Avoiding Seduction in Tonga," in Kulick, Don, and Margaret Willson (eds.), *Taboo: Sex,*

Identity and Erotic Subjectivity in Anthropological Fieldwork, London and New York: Routledge, 168–185.
Muir, Stewart (2004) "Not Quite at Home: Field Envy and New Age Ethnographic Dis-ease," in Hume, Lynne, and Jane Mulcock (eds.), *Anthropologists in the Field: Cases in Participant Observation*, New York: Columbia University Press, 185–200.
Muncey, Tessa (2010) *Creating Autoethnographies*, London and New York: Sage.
Murakami, Haruki (2006) "Nausea 1979," in *Blind Willow, Sleeping Woman*, London: Harvill Secker, 143–153.
Myerhoff, Barbara (1974) *Peyote Hunt: The Sacred Journey of the Huichol Indians*, New York: Cornell University Press.
Norman, Karin (2000) "Phoning the Field: Meanings of Place and Involvement in Fieldwork 'At Home,'" in Amit, Vered (ed.), *Constructing the Field: Ethnographic Fieldwork in the Contemporary World*, London and New York: Routledge, 120–146.
Norris, Clive (1993) "Some Ethical Considerations on Field-Work with the Police," in Hobbs, Dick, and Tim May (eds.), *Interpreting the Field: Accounts of Ethnography*, Oxford and New York: Oxford University Press, 122–135.
Nuttall, Denise (2007) "A Pathway to Knowledge: Embodiment, Dreaming, and Experience as a Basis for Understanding the Other," in Goulet, Jean-Guy A., and Bruce G. Miller (eds.), *Extraordinary Anthropology: Transformations in the Field*, Lincoln and London: The University of Nebraska Press, 323–351.
Ōe, Kenzaburō (1981) *Hiroshima Notes*, translated by David L. Swain and Toshi Yonezawa, New York: Grove Press. Original Edition, 1965.
Okada, Moeko (2012) "Wordplay as a Selling Strategy in Advertisements and Sales Promotions," in Chovanec, Jan, and Isabel Ermida (eds.), *Language and Humour in the Media*, Newcastle upon Tyne: Cambridge Scholars Publishing, 163–182.
Okely, Judith (1996) *Own or Other Culture*, London and New York: Routledge.
Okely, Judith, and Helen Callaway (eds.) (1992) *Anthropology and Autobiography*, London and New York: Routledge.
Okely, Judith (1992) "Anthropology and Autobiography: Participatory Experience and Embodied Knowledge," in Okely, Judith, and Helen Callaway (eds.), *Anthropology and Autobiography*, London and New York: Routledge, 1–27.

Olivier de Sardan, Jean-Pierre (2005) *Anthropology and Development: Understanding Contemporary Social Change*, London and New York: Zed Books.

O'Neill, Martin (2001) "Participation or Observation? Some Practical and Ethical Dilemmas," in Gellner, David N., and Eric Hirsch (eds.), *Inside Organizations: Anthropologists at Work*, Oxford and New York: Berg, 221–230.

Ó Tuathail, Gearóid (1996) *Critical Geopolitics: The Politics of Writing Global Space*, London: Routledge.

Ouroussoff, Alexandra (2001) "What is an Ethnographic Study?" in Gellner, David N., and Eric Hirsch (eds.), *Inside Organizations: Anthropologists at Work*, Oxford and New York: Berg, 35–58.

Pallí Monguilod, Cristina (2001) "Ordering Others and Othering Orders: The Consumption and Disposal of Otherness," in Lee, Nicholas, and Rolland Munro (eds.), *The Consumption of Mass*, Oxford: Blackwell, 189–204.

Parker, Melissa (2001) "Stuck in GUM: An Ethnography of a Clap Clinic," in Gellner, David N., and Eric Hirsch (eds.), *Inside Organizations: Anthropologists at Work*, Oxford and New York: Berg, 137–156.

Perry, John (1989) "Voice-Overs," in Perry, John (ed.), *Doing Fieldwork: Eight Personal Accounts of Social Research*, Sydney: Deakin University Press, 8–23.

Pink, Sarah (2000) "'Informants' Who Come 'Home,'" in Amit, Vered (ed.), *Constructing the Field: Ethnographic Fieldwork in the Contemporary World*, London and New York: Routledge, 96–119.

Pihlström, Sami (2011) *Transcendental Guilt: Reflections on Ethical Finitude*, Lanham: Lexington Books.

Piolat, Jérémie (2011) *Portrait du Colonialiste: L'Effet Boomerang de sa Violence et de ses Destructions*, Paris: La Découverte.

Plumelle-Uribe, Rosa Amelia (2001) *La Férocité Blanche: Des Non-Blancs aux Non-Aryens, Ces Génocides Occultés de 1492 à nos Jours*, Paris: Albin Michel.

Pons, Philippe (2012) "Drôle Comme un Japonais," *Le Monde*, November 03, 2012.

Poe, Edgar Allan (1846) "The Philosophy of Composition," *Graham's Magazine*, XXVIII (4): 28: 163–167.

Powdermaker, Hortense (1967) *Stranger and Friend: The Way of an Anthropologist*, London: Secker and Warburg.

Rabinow, Paul (2008) *Marking Time: On the Anthropology of the Contemporary*, Princeton: Princeton University Press.
Rabinow, Paul (1977) *Reflections on Fieldwork in Morocco*, Berkeley: University of California Press.
Rabinow, Paul, and George E. Marcus (2008) *Designs for an Anthropology of the Contemporary*, Durham and London: Duke University Press.
Rabinow, Paul, and William M. Sullivan (1979) *Interpretive Social Science: A Reader*, Berkeley: University of California Press.
Rapport, Nigel (2003) *I am Dynamite: An Alternative Anthropology of Power*, London: Routledge.
Rapport, Nigel (2000) "The Narrative as Fieldwork Technique: Processual Ethnography for a World in Motion," in Amit, Vered (ed.), *Constructing the Field: Ethnographic Fieldwork in the Contemporary World*, London and New York: Routledge, 71–95.
Reed-Danahay, Deborah (1997) *Auto/Ethnography: Rewriting the Self and the Social*, Oxford and New York: Berg.
Rethmann, Petra (2007) "On Presence," in Goulet, Jean-Guy A., and Bruce G. Miller (eds.), *Extraordinary Anthropology: Transformations in the Field*, Lincoln and London: The University of Nebraska Press, 36–54.
Ribeiro, Gustavo Lins, and Arturo Escobar (eds.) (2008) *Antropologías del Mundo: Transformaciones Disciplinarias dentro de Sistemas de Poder*, Popayán: Envión Editores.
Ricoeur, Paul (1969) *Le Conflit des Interprétations*, Paris: Seuil.
Rivière, Peter (2010) "Alfred Métraux: Empiricist and Romanticist," in Parkin, Robert, and Anne de Sales (eds.), *Out of the Study and into the Field: Ethnographic Theory and Practice in French Anthropology*, New York and Oxford: Berghahn Books, 151–169.
Robben, A. C. G. M. (1996) "Ethnographic Seduction, Transference, and Resistance in Dialogues about Terror and Violence in Argentina," *Ethos*, 24 (1): 71–106.
Robben, Antonius C. G. M., and Jeffrey A. Sluka (eds.) (2007) *Ethnographic Fieldwork: An Anthropological Reader*, Malden, Oxford, and Carlton: Blackwell Publishing.
Robinson, Gary (2004) "Living in Sheds: Suicide, Friendship, and Research among the Tiwi," in Hume, Lynne, and Jane Mulcock (eds.), *Anthropologists in the Field: Cases in Participant Observation*, New York: Columbia University Press, 153–167.

Rock, Paul (2007) "Symbolic Interactionism and Ethnography," in Atkinson, Paul, et al. (eds.), *Handbook of Ethnography*, London: Sage, 26–39.
Rosaldo, Renato (1993) *Culture and Truth: The Remaking of Social Analysis*, London: Routledge. Original Edition, 1989.
Sade, D. A. F. de. (1990) *Œuvres. Tome 1*, Bibliothèque de la pléiade, Paris: Gallimard.
Sade, D. A. F. de. (1995) *Œuvres. Tome 2*, Bibliothèque de la pléiade, Paris: Gallimard.
Sade, D. A. F. de. (1998) *Œuvres. Tome 3*, Bibliothèque de la pléiade, Paris: Gallimard.
Said, Edward W. (1978) *Orientalism*, New York: Pantheon Books.
Sartre, Jean-Paul (1981) *Œuvres Romanesques*, Bibliothèque de la pléiade, Paris: Gallimard.
Sartre, Jean-Paul (2000) *Huis Clos, suivi de Les Mouches*, Paris: Gallimard. Original Edition, 1947.
Scheper-Hughes, Nancy (2000) "Ire in Ireland," *Ethnography*, 1 (1): 17–40.
Scheper-Hughes, Nancy (2001) *Saints, Scholars, and Schizophrenics: Mental Illness in Rural Ireland*, Berkeley and London: The University of California Press. Original Edition, 1979.
Schroeder, Christopher (2004) "The Ethnographic Experience of Postmodern Literacies," in Brown, Stephen Gilbert, and Sidney I. Dobrin (eds.), *Ethnography Unbound: From Theory Shock to Critical Praxis*, New York: State University of New York Press, 53–72.
Searles, Ned (2006) "Anthropology in an Era of Inuit Empowerment," in Stern, Pamela, and Lisa Stevenson (eds.), *Critical Inuit Studies: An Anthology of Contemporary Arctic Ethnography*, Lincoln and London: University of Nebraska Press, 89–101.
Segalen, Victor (1978) *Essai sur l'Exotisme: Une Esthétique du Divers*, Saint-Clément-de-Rivière: Fata Morgana.
Shankman, Paul (2009) *The Trashing of Margaret Mead: Anatomy of an Anthropological Controversy*, Madison: The University of Wisconsin Press.
Shuttleworth, Russell (2004) "Multiple Roles, Statuses, and Allegiances: Exploring the Ethnographic Process in Disability Culture," in Hume, Lynne, and Jane Mulcock (eds.), *Anthropologists in the Field: Cases in Participant Observation*, New York: Columbia University Press, 46–58.
Shostak, Marjorie (2000) *Nisa: The Life and Words of a !Kung Woman*, Cambridge, Mass.: Harvard University Press. Original Edition, 1981.

Silverman, David (1997) *Qualitative Research: Theory, Method, and Practice*, London and Thousand Oaks: Sage.
Sōseki, Natsume (1968) *The Three-Cornered World*, Tokyo: Charles E. Tuttle. Original Edition, 1906.
Spivak, Gayatri Chakravorty (1988) "Can the Subaltern Speak?" in Nelson, Cary, and Larry Grossberg (eds.), *Marxism and the Interpretation of Culture*, Chicago: University of Illinois Press, 271–313.
Stewart, Kathleen (2007) *Ordinary Affects*, New York: Duke University Press.
Stewart, Kathleen (1996) *A Space on the Side of the Road: Cultural Poetics in an "Other" America*, Princeton: Princeton University Press.
Stoller, Paul (1989) *The Taste of Ethnographic Things*, Philadelphia: University of Pennsylvania Press.
Suzuki, Tomi (1996) *Narrating the Self: Fictions of Japanese Modernity*, Stanford: Stanford University Press.
Taussig, Michael T. (2003) "The Diary as Witness: An Anthropologist Writes What He Must," *The Chronicle of Higher Education*, December 19.
Taussig, Michael T. (1992) *The Nervous System*, New York and London: Routledge.
Taussig, Michael T. (2010) *The Devil and Commodity Fetishism in South America*, Chapel Hill: The University of North Carolina Press. Original Edition, 1980.
Thomas, Jim (1992) *Doing Critical Ethnography*, London and New York: Sage.
Todorov, Tzvetan (1992) *Nous et les Autres: La Réflexion Française sur la Diversité Humaine*, Paris: Seuil.
Turner, Victor W., and Edward M. Bruner (eds.) (1986) *The Anthropology of Experience*.
Turner, Victor (1985) *On the Edge of the Bush: Anthropology as Experience*, Tucson: The University of Arizona Press.
Turner, Victor (1975) *Revelation and Divination in Ndembu Ritual*, Ithaca and New York: Cornell University Press.
Tyler, Stephen A. (1987) *The Unspeakable: Discourse, Dialogue, and Rhetoric in the Postmodern World*, Madison: University of Wisconsin Press.
Tyler, Stephen A. (1992) "On Being Out of Words," in Marcus, George E. (ed.), *Rereading Cultural Anthropology*, Durham: Duke University Press, 1–7.
Urry, John (2002) *The Tourist Gaze*, London: Sage.

van den Berghe, Pierre L., and Charles F. Keys (1984) "Introduction: Tourism and Re-created Ethnicity," *Annals of Tourism Research*, 11 (3): 343–352.

Van Gennep, Arnold (1981) *Les Rites de Passage*, Paris: Picard. Original Edition 1909.

Van Maanen, John (ed.) (1995) *Representation in Ethnography*, Thousand Oaks: Sage.

Van Maanen, John (1988) *Tales of the Field: On Writing Ethnography*, Chicago: University of Chicago Press.

Wachowich, Nancy (2006) "Cultural Survival and the Trade in Iglulingmiut Traditions," in Stern, Pamela, and Lisa Stevenson (eds.), *Critical Inuit Studies: An Anthology of Contemporary Arctic Ethnography*, Lincoln and London: University of Nebraska Press, 119–138.

Warf, Barney (2008) *Time-Space Compression: Historical Geographies*, London and New York: Routledge.

Wilkes, Barbara (2007) "Reveal or Conceal," in Goulet, Jean-Guy A., and Bruce G. Miller (eds.), *Extraordinary Anthropology: Transformations in the Field*, Lincoln and London: The University of Nebraska Press, 53–84.

Winnicott, Donald W. (1958) "Hate in the Countertransference," *Through Paediatrics to Psycho-Analysis: Collected Papers*, London: Tavistock, 194–203. Original Edition, 1947.

Wolcott, Harry F. (2005) *The Art of Fieldwork*, Walnut Creek: AltaMira Press.

Wolcott, Harry F. (2002) *Sneaky Kid and Its Aftermath: Ethics and Intimacy in Fieldwork*, Walnut Creek: AltaMira Press.

Yan, Geling (2006) *The Uninvited*, London: Faber and Faber Limited.

Index

autobiography, 23

Bataille, Georges, 81

cannibalism, 41
Céline, Louis-Ferdinand, 85
colonialism, 16

ethnogastritis, 2, 15, 68, 70, 78, 80, 87, 90, 98

exoticism, 5, 19, 42, 52

reflexivity, 22

Sartre, Jean-Paul, 63
shame, 14

tourism, 19

vertigo, 84